NUTSHELL

E.U. LAW
IN A NUTSHELL

AUSTRALIA
Law Book Co.
Sydney

CANADA and USA
Carswell
Toronto

HONG KONG
Sweet & Maxwell Asia

NEW ZEALAND
Brookers
Wellington

SINGAPORE and MALAYSIA
Sweet & Maxwell Asia
Singapore and Kuala Lumpur

NUTSHELLS

E.U. LAW
IN A NUTSHELL

FOURTH EDITION

by

Mike Cuthbert, LL.M., BSc.(Econ.),B.A.(Law)
Senior Tutor in Law,
University College Northampton

London • Sweet & Maxwell • 2003

First Edition 1994
Second Edition 1997
Third Edition 2000
Fourth Edition 2003

Published by Sweet & Maxwell Limited of
100 Avenue Road, Swiss Cottage, London, NW3 3PF
www.sweetandmaxwell.co.uk
Phototypeset by
LBJ Typesetting Ltd of Kingsclere
Printed in Great Britain by CPD Wales, Ebbw Vale

No natural forests were destroyed to make this product:
only farmed timber was used and replanted

ISBN 0 421 78380 X

**A CIP Catalogue record for this book
is available from the British Library**

CONTENTS

1. THE EUROPEAN COMMUNITY INSTITUTIONS

When the Treaty of European Union (TEU) came into force on November 1, 1993 it became legally correct to refer to the European Community (EC). The word "economic" was dropped to reflect the fact that there has been a change of emphasis towards non-economic provisions such as citizenship. It also became usual to refer to the European Union at the expense of the European Community. There were originally three Communities, with the European Coal & Steel Community (ECSC) being established in 1952 and the EC together with EURATOM coming in 1957. However, the ECSC had a fixed life of 50 years so ceased to exist in 2002. The policy areas of coal and steel have been subsumed into the EC Treaty. Thus we now have two Communities, but the European Community is the most important pillar of the EU and the EC Treaty, as amended by the TEU, still dominates. This will be observed in this book as you will see repeated reference to the EC Treaty. (Chapter 11 looks at the TEU and its subsequent amendment by the Treaty of Amsterdam and the Treaty of Nice in more detail, see p.100).

In 1952 the first of the European Communities was established in the form of the European Coal and Steel Community (ECSC). Although this had followed on from other bodies established by an international agreement, such as the Council of Europe (1949), the development of this Community was characterised by a clear transfer of rights to special institutions. These rights had been previously seen as sovereign to national governments. In 1957 the European Economic Community (now simply the European Community under the Treaty on European Union) and EURATOM were established. Initially the three European Communities had different institutions and in the case of the Commission a different name in the sense that for the purposes of the ECSC it was called the High Authority. This was all changed by the Merger Treaty of 1965 which made the institutions common to all three Communities. Although the powers and procedures for these institutions may vary from one Treaty to another, it is now common to refer to the European Community as one community with the dominance of the European Community Treaty.

EUROPEAN PARLIAMENT

It is Pt 5 of the EC Treaty which lays out the "Provision Governing the Institutions". The first institution dealt with is the European Parliament (EP), although it was initially referred to as the European Assembly. Perhaps, given the democratic underpinning which is now explicitly stated in the TEU, we now assume this to be essential for the EC. But the original Parliament was not democratically elected nor did it fulfil any of the functions we might identify as the characteristics of a parliament, of any tradition. The membership was nominated by the governments of the Member States (MS) to exercise advisory and supervisory powers. However, its place as the first institution in Pt 5 may have more significance for the "vision" of Europe shared by the authors of the Treaty. The current discussion between those who see the Community as having a purely economic function as against those with a wider political "federal" viewpoint have their philosophical base in the Treaty. The original Parliament was very weak because the establishment and success of the EC depended upon a strong role for the governments of the MS and thus the Council of Ministers. However, having recognised the need for a "democratic" institution in the Treaty it was possible to strengthen its powers and thus its role over time. This is what happened and is happening with regard to the European Parliament.

It is the amended Arts 189–201 EC (ex 137–144 EC) that provide the foundation for the European Parliament. Direct elections specified under Art.190(3) (ex 138(3)) have taken place every five years since 1979. The number of representatives to be elected in each MS is as shown in Table 1.1 below.

Table 1.1 Number of Representatives by Member State

Austria	21
Belgium	25
Denmark	16
Finland	16
France	87
Germany	99
Greece	25
Ireland	15
Italy	87
Luxembourg	6

Netherlands	31
Portugal	25
Spain	64
Sweden	22
United Kingdom	87

Source: Art.190 EC

The original delegates, nominated by Member States, have been replaced by Members of the European Parliament (MEPs) who represent their constituents. All elections to the European Parliament are based on the principle of proportional representation, unlike under the normal British principle of "first past the post". This led to the novel introduction on the British mainland of the results of the 1999 European Parliamentary elections being based on a "list" system rather than the traditional "one MEP–one constituency" of previous elections in Britain. Since the introduction of direct elections in 1979 it is obvious that the character of the European Parliament has changed. This is reflected not only in the procedures that the MEPs have adopted for themselves where they have become more professional, but also in the demands they have made to increase their role and powers within the Community. MEPs basically want to have the role of a "parliament". Although this concept varies between the Member States, the common characteristic is the role in the legislative process and the accountability of the "government" to the MEPs. There is no "government" in the national sense within the EC, thus the emphasis has been on the involvement in the legislative process. The Single European Act (SEA) recognised this and introduced the co-operation procedure. The Treaty on European Union took this a step further with the co-decision procedure and the subsequent Treaty of Amsterdam and Treaty of Nice have consolidated this development.

DECISION-MAKING PROCEDURES

The role of the European Parliament is increasing as it now participates more fully in the legislative process associated with Art.249 EC (ex 189 EC). Article 192 EC (ex 138(b)) gives the EP the authority to request the Commission to submit any appropriate proposal on matters that it considers that the Community should act. Previously this was something only the Council of

Ministers could do under Art.208 EC (ex 152 EC). Requests have to be made to the European Commission because under the Treaty they are given the role of initiator.

As a result of increasing the powers of the European Parliament the Community's decision-making procedures became very complex. There were six decision-making procedures which varied with the area of legislation under consideration, however these have now been simplified by the Treaty of Amsterdam.

Consultation: This is the original procedure with a single Parliamentary reading which was laid down by the EC Treaty in 1957. The voting in the Council of Ministers has to be unanimous.

Co-operation: (Art.252 EC (ex 189(c) EC)) This procedure was introduced by the Single European Act 1987. It requires two Parliamentary readings and qualified majority voting in the Council. (See Chapter 2 below, p.19). Its role has been restricted by the Treaty of Amsterdam to areas of European Monetary Union (EMU).

Co-decision: (Art.251 EC (ex 189(b) EC)) This is the most recent and most important procedure with regard to legislation, introduced by the TEU in 1993 and extensively developed by the Treaty of Amsterdam and the Treaty of Nice. Under this procedure the Parliament is given the power to prevent legislation being adopted. Generally qualified majority voting is required in the Council except on two issues where unanimity applies. (See Chapter 2 below, p.19). Examples of policy areas now under the co-decision procedure include: transport policy; development aid; Trans-European Networks; employment policy; public health; and equal opportunities.

Assent: This procedure was originally introduced by the SEA, but its scope has been increased by the TEU. It applies in the case of international agreements, Treaty decisions and accession of new members.

Budget: This is covered by a procedure in Arts 272–276 EC (ex 203–206 EC), which gives some authority to the European Parliament. See the EP and the Community Budget below, p.6.

However, whatever weight is given to the views of the European Parliament, its right to be consulted must be respected. Failure to follow this procedural requirement may lead to the measure being declared invalid. This happened in the cases of Case 138/79 *Roquette v Council* and Case 139/79 *Maizena v Council*, both reported in 1980.

The European Parliament has certain characteristics similar to national parliaments. There are a number of standing committees that mirror the major policy areas of the Community. These committees carry out investigations and hear evidence from experts and interested parties, including the Commission. They also issue reports. In addition parliamentary questions are an important element of control over the Commission. Under Art.197 (ex 140) of the EC Treaty the Commission must reply orally or in writing to questions put to it by MEPs. In fact the Council and foreign ministers also take part in this process. It is common practice now for the President of the Council of Ministers to make a report to the Parliament at the end of their term as President.

European Ombudsman

As with national parliaments, those who are affected by particular policies or proposals can complain to their representative. The Treaty on European Union allows for such petitions to be made to their MEP (Art.195 EC (ex 138(e) EC)). In addition there is now provision for the appointment by the EP of an Ombudsman to deal with complaints from any citizen of the Union, including those undertakings with a registered office in a Member State. The complaints can deal with any instances of maladministration. This encompasses the activities of all Community institutions and bodies, excluding the ECJ and CFI when acting in their judicial role.

European Parliament and the Commission

The Treaty made the European Commission responsible to the European Parliament. Once appointed by the Member States and approved by the European Parliament, the 20 Commissioners can only be removed by the EP passing a censure motion by a two-thirds majority vote and an absolute majority of its members under Art.201 EC. Such a motion successfully passed would force the resignation of the whole Commission.

Although threatened on occasion this has never happened, although in order to avoid the motion of censure the Commission can resign, as it did on March 16, 1999. (See "Commissioners" below, p.10).

European Parliament and the Community Budget

The right of the European Parliament to make changes in the budget depends on the distinction between expenditure which is "compulsory" and other expenditure which is "non-compulsory". Compulsory expenditure covers that expenditure which is committed under Treaty provisions or Community legislation, *e.g.* the Common Agricultural Policy. Parliament can only propose modifications to this category of expenditure, thus giving the Council the final say in such matters. However, non-compulsory expenditure which includes all expenditure which is not the inevitable consequences of Community legislation, can be amended by the majority of MEPs voting in favour of such proposals. This expenditure includes the Community social policy, regional and industrial policies, and accounts for about 39 per cent of the total Community budget. For this type of expenditure it is the European Parliament that has the final control. Therefore, although the Parliament does have some powers of approval as far as the budget is concerned, these are weak with regard to compulsory expenditure, which is the vast majority of the total budget.

In 1975 the European Parliament was given increased powers in relation to the Community budget by a conciliation procedure. The aim of these powers was to give the Parliament more effective participation in the budgetary process, by seeking agreement between the Parliament and the Council of Ministers. If the Parliament refuses to pass the budget as presented to it by the Council, a number of important consequences follow. First the budget cannot be implemented, which has implications for the expenditure level of the Community which is limited to one-twelfth of the previous year's budget per month. Secondly a "conciliation committee", consisting of the Council and representatives of the European Parliament is established to try to resolve the disagreement. The European Commission assists the work of the committee.

Ultimately the Parliament may reject the budget outright under Art.272 (ex 203 EC) of the EC Treaty by a two-thirds vote cast by a majority of its members. Although it may reject it, the

Parliament cannot increase the total amount of the budget beyond the maximum rate of increase set by the Commission, unless the alteration is agreed by the Council. In 1988, in an attempt to improve the budgetary procedure, an Institutional Agreement was entered into by the Council, Commission and the European Parliament. While recognising the varying competencies of the institutions in the budgetary field, it fixed new rules for co-operation between the institutions.

Council of Ministers

The Council of Ministers is specified in Arts 202–210 EC (ex 145–154 EC). This is the main political institution of the EC. Its membership is made up of one representative of each of the 15 Member States. Although the main representative is the foreign minister of each Member State, the actual minister varies with the main business of the meeting. Thus if the Common Agricultural Policy is being discussed it will be the agricultural ministers who will attend and so on. The presidency of the Council is held in rotation by each Member State for a period of six months. The representative of the Member State holding the Presidency will always chair the meetings during this period. This has been criticised on the grounds that the period is too short for individual ministers to acquire expertise in the role.

Voting Procedures However, the main discussion and action involving the Council of Ministers has centred on its voting procedures. In the EC Treaty it was envisaged that the Council would move, after the transitional period, to majority voting except for those specific matters identified by the Treaty as requiring unanimity. This was not to be a simple majority but a qualified one on the basis of Art.205 EC (ex 148 EC). This article gives each Member State a number of votes depending roughly upon the size of its population but with a minimum of two votes for the smallest country, Luxembourg. The "big four" of France, Germany, Italy and the UK have 10 votes. On any issue before the Council it requires a combination of the larger and smaller Member States to accumulate the necessary votes to adopt the measure. This seeks to ensure that no interest group in the Council can dominate the voting and encourages a compromise in the sense that the measure must be acceptable to a range of Member States. The necessary voting majority at present is 62 in favour of the measure. In preparation for enlargement in 2004 the Treaty of Nice has also introduced the possibility of a member of the Council requesting that such a majority vote also constitutes 62 per cent of the total population of the EU. (See Chapter 11—The TEU and Beyond, p.100).

'Veto'   The intention of the Treaty was hindered by the events of 1966 which led to the Luxembourg Accord or Compromise, which was instituted to obtain the co-operation of the French Government in the working of the EC. This recognition of a "veto" in the sense that unanimity was required on particular issues not specified as requiring them under the Treaty, slowed down the actions of the Council in that it could not proceed faster than its slowest participating government. The governments of Denmark, Ireland, the UK, Greece, Portugal and Spain who joined in the 1970s and 1980s assumed that they did so with a power of veto on issues they considered important to them. Although they were politically shocked on occasions when they were thwarted in their attempts to exercise it, it was not until the Single European Act that attempts were made to speed up the decision-making process of the Council. For example, Art.100(a), the article providing the legal base for adopting the measures necessary for the establishment and functioning of the internal market, was passed to meet the target date of January 1, 1993 for completing this objective. Although academic debate still continues on whether the veto still exists, it is important to recognise the political nature of the Council. If the President of the Council is aware of the political implications of calling for a vote where a minority of the Council have strong objections, it is likely that such a vote will be postponed for further discussion.

Democratic Control

If the European Parliament, as indicated above, wishes to exercise more authority in the legislative process it has to be at a reduction of that held by the Council. Some politicians see the control of national parliaments over their government ministers as being the democratic control element of the Community. Such politicians see the European Parliament as a weak alternative and do not welcome changes to the relationship with the Council which they feel weakens the status of the Member State governments. In the UK the analogy is of the Westminster Parliament becoming like a county or local council in relation to the European Parliament.

However, is it realistic to expect the government ministers to play a significant role in developing policy as against making decisions to adopt such policies or legislation? If you look at any British minister who may be involved in a meeting of the Council of Ministers, he is in charge of a government department and takes part in debates and answers questions in the House of Commons or in exceptional cases the House of Lords. As an MP there are constituent problems and interests to deal with. How much time is there for EC matters? Obviously there has to be some time because it is part of the minister's job, but a great deal of the work of the Council of Ministers is undertaken by the Committee of Permanent Representatives or COREPER.

Committee of Permanent Representatives (COREPER)

This group of diplomats represent the views or interests of their particular government. They liase with the various government ministries and bring these views to the discussions which take place in Brussels. The idea is that when the Council of Ministers meet much of the preliminary discussion has taken place and the Ministers can concentrate on those issues which may require a political compromise or are politically sensitive. Thus the Council's agenda will have "A" items, which have already been agreed in principle and "B" items where further discussion by the ministers is necessary to get agreement.

European Commission

The European Commissioners are sometimes described as a kind of European civil servant. However, this is too simplistic. Civil servants are expected to carry out the wishes of their political masters. Although the European Commission acts as the executive of the EC by implementing the policies decided by the Council and the European Parliament, they make proposals as to what those policies should be. Such proposals made by the Commissions are not always welcomed by the Council in the sense that they take a European stance against the perceived interests of the individual Member States. Much of the impetus for the legislation for the completion of the internal market came from the Commission. There are also examples where the authority of the EC has been extended to the embarrassment of some Member States, *e.g.* the directives dealing with beaches or water purity.

Commissioners There are 20 Commissioners in total, with two each nominated from Germany, France, Italy, the UK and Spain and one each from the other countries. It usual for Commissioners to have held high political office in their national governments. However, once appointed they are required to act independently. From January 7, 1995 the term of office was extended to five years, to synchronise with the term of the European Parliament. Commissioners can be re-appointed. Under the Maastricht Treaty Parliament must approve the appointment of the Commission and be consulted by the Member States before the President is nominated. This has been strengthened by the Treaty of Amsterdam which now requires the EP to approve the appointment of the President of the Commission (see Art.214 EC). The President-elect of the Commission must then be consulted by the Member States before they nominate the remaining Commissioners (Art.214 EC (ex 158 EC)). Although the Commission acts as a collegiate body, each Commissioner is allocated a portfolio from the 20 directorate-generals covering all Community policies. From enlargement in 2004 no Member State will be allowed to nominate more than one Commissioner. (See Chapter 11 TEU and Beyond, p.100).

Duties of the Commission Articles 211 to 219 EC (ex 155–163 EC) deal with the European Commission. It is Art.211 EC (ex 155 EC) that shows the wide range of duties imposed on the Commission. The Commission initiate policies by making proposals, but they also act as the executive arm of the Community once a proposal has been adopted by an administrative act under Art.249 EC (ex 189 EC). They are the "guardians of the Treaty". This covers not only questions concerning the relationship between the institutions, but more specifically the Enforcement Action under Art.226 EC (ex 169 EC) and Competition Policy of the EC. Both of these topics are dealt with in Chapter 7, p.68.

European Court of Justice

The European Court of Justice is the final main institution of the EC and fulfils the judicial role necessary to ensure that Community law is observed. In fact Art.220 EC (ex 164 EC) is very short and states "The Court of Justice shall ensure that in the interpretation and application of this Treaty the law is observed." This is achieved via specific direct and indirect actions, which are discussed in the chapters dealing with Preliminary References and Judicial Review (Chapter 5, p.47). However, the important points to note at this stage are the membership and procedures of the ECJ. The main influences at the early formative years of the Court were the German but more predominantly the French legal tradition. This is shown not only in the fact that the working language of the Court is French but more importantly in the office of Advocate Generals.

Judges There are 15 judges on the ECJ with each Member State providing one judge. Appointed for a term of six years, the judges elect their own President of the Court who serves in that post for three years. Like all posts within the Court it is possible for the period in office to be renewed. Although this fixed but renewable term of office is not found in English courts, the attributes the judges should have are the same. Article 223 EC (ex 167 EC) specifies that "they should be independent and qualified for the highest judicial office within their respective countries". However, an important difference is that whereas English judges are selected from barristers and to a lesser extent solicitors, judges in some Member States are chosen from a much wider field, including academic lawyers. Thus when the judges in the European Court deliberate they are bringing together a variety of legal backgrounds which would not be found in an English court.

Advocates-General The post of Advocate-General, is derived from the French legal system and unknown in English law. There are eight Advocate-Generals appointed to the Court. They have the same backgrounds as judges, the same term of office and perhaps most importantly the same status. Therefore Advocate-Generals should not be seen as inferior to judges, as the precedent within the Court for both depends upon the date of appointment and not the designated office. Advocate-Generals are given a specific role under Art.222 EC (ex 166 EC) which states that "it should be the duty of the Advocate-General, acting with complete impartiality and independence, to make, in open court, reasoned submissions on cases brought before the Court of Justice, in order to assist the Court in the performance of" its tasks.

Judgments Unlike in senior English courts where a full judgment is given, including dissenting views, only one judgment is given by the ECJ. All the judges must agree to the one judgment which is why they can appear so terse and lacking in any real discussion of the Law. They do not contain the *obiter dicta* as well as the *ratio decidendi* found in the common law tradition. Hence the importance of the Advocate-General is that he hears and reads all the evidence as a judge would do but he gives his opinion to the court as to what the judgment should be before the judges themselves reach their decision. In his opinion the Advocate-General can range over the case law of the court or if appropriate the jurisprudence of the Member States. In this way some insight is given as to the direction European Community Law may take in the future.

Workload   The workload of the ECJ has increased tremendously since the Court was established in 1957. To help the court deal with cases, the judges sit in Chambers of up to five judges, but always with an odd number so that there can be a clear decision in the case. In 1989 the Court of First Instance (CFI) was set up to assist the ECJ by taking a specific jurisdiction with the safeguard of appeal to the ECJ itself. The ECJ itself has a general jurisdiction with regard to Community Law only fettered by the types of action specified in the Treaty. There are a number of direct actions available that include judicial review (Art.230 EC (ex 173 EC)) and actions against a Member State for failure to fulfil an obligation (Arts 226 and 227 EC (ex 169 and 170 EC)). In addition there is the special procedure for preliminary references under Art.234 EC (ex 177 EC).

Procedures   Whenever a case is brought to the ECJ, whether as a direct action which is heard in its entirety only by the Court or a request for a preliminary reference from a Member State under Art.234 EC (ex 177 EC), it is processed by the Court Registry to ensure that the progress of the case can be recorded. This is especially important with preliminary references where the whole procedure is dominated by the "file" of written documentation sent by the national court. The procedure is that on receipt by the Registrar, the President of the Court will assign the case to one of the Chambers and nominate one of the judges to act as "rapporteur". The First Advocate-General will at the same time designate the Advocate-General for the case. The role of the judge rapporteur is that although all the papers will go to every judge hearing the case, only he will have studied them closely in order to produce a preliminary report. This report, together with any views expressed by the Advocate-General will help the court decide what the relevant issues are. It may be decided that the case should be heard by the full court, as normally happens with cases between the Member States or Community institutions. These early stages covering the written proceedings and the preparatory inquiry are held in private. Where oral proceedings follow, as with direct actions, these are held in open court in Luxembourg. The next stage is for the Advocate-General to deliver his opinion to the court. Some time after this the court will deliver its judgment.

The Future   The President of the ECJ has presented to the Justice Ministers of the Member States a number of proposals and ideas on the future of the judicial system of the EU. Principally he thought that the judicial system would be affected by an increase in the volume of cases due to the Economic Monetary Union (EMU), the full implementation of the Treaty of Amsterdam and the enlargement of the EU. The ECJ wants to avoid the situation where case congestion leads to growing delays by simplifying procedures and filtering appeals from the CFI. The Court is also concerned with the increase in the number of judges associated with enlargement and a loss of its collegiate function. The Treaty of Nice has provided some solutions to these issues.

Court of First Instance (CFI)

This Court was established under the Single European Act (SEA) and came into operation in 1989. The CFI is attached to the ECJ and has a wide jurisdiction with a possible appeal to the ECJ itself. The SEA uses the word "attach" quite deliberately. The CFI is not a separate institution. It shares not only the building in Luxembourg with the ECJ but other facilities such as the library. It appoints its own Registrar but other administrative services are shared.

The CFI is based on Art.225 EC (ex 168(a) EC). There are 15 judges appointed to the court, one from each Member State. Although there are no Advocate-Generals specifically appointed to the CFI the need for such a role to be fulfilled is recognised. Where an Advocate-General is required in a particular case, one of the judges is requested to carry out this role. This will not happen in every case before the CFI. The court may sit in chambers of three or five judges in order to hear cases brought before it.

Like the judges appointed to the ECJ, those appointed to the CFI have a six-year term of office, which is renewable. Unlike their colleagues, the criteria for selection as a judge in the CFI is not so high as the ECJ. In the ECJ prospective judges must possess the ability for appointment to high judicial office. Article 225 EC (ex 168(a)(3) EC) states that for the CFI, judges are to be chosen "from persons whose independence is beyond doubt and who possess the ability required for appointment to judicial office".

Jurisdiction   The initial jurisdiction of the CFI indicated that one of the problems encountered by the ECJ was those cases that required a long examination of questions of fact. These are very time consuming and involve sifting through a great deal of evidence. There were three categories of cases which formed the original jurisdiction of the CFI:

(1) Staff cases, where employees of the Committee have a dispute with regard to their employment;
(2) cases brought under the European Coal and Steel Community Treaty concerned with production and prices; and
(3) most importantly, competition cases brought under either Art.230 EC (ex 173 EC) or Art.232 EC (ex 175 EC).

If these cases also contain a claim for damages, the CFI can hear that claim as part of the action. Appeals from the CFI are to the ECJ and have to be brought within two months. The appeal will only be heard on points of law and not of fact. The three grounds of appeal mirror the grounds of annulment under Art.230 EC (ex 173 EC), namely lack of competence; breach of procedure; or infringement of Community law by the Court of First Instance.

In September 1993 there was the first major increase in the jurisdiction of the Court since its creation in 1988. The Council of Ministers extended the jurisdiction to cover all direct actions brought by private parties against the Community institutions. However, this does not as yet apply to anti-dumping cases. One of the main purposes for the extension of the CFI jurisdiction is to permit the ECJ to reduce still further delays in hearing cases by cutting the court's case load. However, the ECJ will take on the role as the appeal court for all the cases transferred to the

CFI – all cases heard by the CFI at first instance may be appealed to the ECJ on a point of law. The CFI does not have competence to hear references for preliminary ruling under Art.234 EC (ex 177 EC) under the existing treaties but the Treaty of Nice does allow for this to happen after 2004. (See Chapter 11 TEU and Beyond, p.100).

Court of Auditors

There has been such a Court since the EC was established and therefore changes in the TEU should be regarded as an upgrading of its status generated by the need to monitor the large budgets now controlled by the Community.

The duty of the Court of Auditors is to carry out audits of all revenue and expenditure of the Community and the bodies set up by the Community. It must provide the Parliament and the Council with a statement that transactions have been legally made and that the accounts produced are accurate. At the end of the financial year the Court of Auditors has to draw up an annual report which is presented to the other Community institutions for their observations. These and the report are then published in the Official Journal.

There are 15 members of the Court of Auditors each serving for a six-year period which is reviewable. To facilitate an overlap in membership four members of the Court are to be appointed for four years only. The members of the Court elect their own President, who serves for a period of three years.

It is the Council, after consulting the Parliament, which appoints the members of the Court of Auditors. Apart from the end of their period in office or death, the Court of Justice can terminate the office of a member at the request of the Court of Auditors if he no longer fulfils the obligations of his office.

The audits carried out by the Court of Auditors can be carried out on the spot in the other institutions of the Community and the Member States. Where it takes place in the Member States they liase with the national audit bodies, who may take part in the audit. All the Community institutions and national audit bodies must forward to the Court of Auditors any document or information it requests to carry out its task.

Advisory Institutions

There are also advisory bodies with the power to give opinions either in cases where they have been consulted by the Council or Commission or in cases where they consider it appropriate.

The Economic and Social Committee was established by the EC Treaty in 1957. A new one, the Committee of the Regions, was established by the TEU.

Economic and Social Committee

This is an advisory committee appointed under Arts 257 and 262 EC (ex 193 and 198 EC). It consists of representatives of the various sections of economic and social life of the Community. Although the opinions of the Committee are not binding they do appear to have influence. The Commission has a very good working relationship with the Economic and Council Committee. The relationship with the Council has not been so well developed although attempts have been made in recent years to improve this. Since 1987 it has become a regular practice for the person holding the office of President of the Council to address the Committee on matters discussed at the European Council. This has spread to ministers from the member state holding the Presidency to address meetings of the Committee.

Although advisory, the Commission or Council consult the Committee when it considers it appropriate in addition to those instances where it is obligatory under some articles of the Treaty for the Council or the Commission to consult the Committee. An example of this is Art.71 EC (ex 75 EC) which deals with international transport within the Community and the common rules established to implement the policy.

There are a total of 222 members of the Economic and Social Committee. These are allocated to the different Member States to reflect their size, with the large countries such as France, Italy, Germany and the UK having 24 each, down to six for Luxembourg. The Committee reflects three particular groups of people. The Employers Group which is made up of representatives of employers organisations and chambers of commerce; the Workers Group which represent trade unions; and a group of "Other Interests" which includes small businesses, family, environmental and similar representatives. Within these groups can be found the representatives of the various categories of economic and social activity specified in Art.257 EC (ex 193EC).

Committee of the Regions

This Committee consists of representatives of regional and local bodies. The number of members from each Member State is given in Table 1.2 below, p.17:

Table 1.2 Committee of the Regions, Number of Representatives by Member States

Austria	12
Belgium	12
Denmark	9
Finland	9
France	24
Germany	24
Greece	12
Ireland	9
Italy	24
Luxembourg	6
Netherlands	12
Portugal	12
Spain	21
Sweden	12
UK	24

Source: Art.263 EC

The individual Member States propose their members who are appointed by the Council for four years, which is renewable. The members have a duty to act independently, in the general interest of the Community. In view of the expansion of the Community's Structural Funds and the creation of a Cohesion Fund to redress the imbalance of prosperity within the Community, it is likely that this new Committee will make an important contribution to the Community's decision-making.

Institutional Reforms

Apart from the European Parliament, the main institutions have remained largely unchanged since the Treaty of Rome, yet the size and policies of the EC have been greatly enlarged. This has caused the present main institutions to creak and struggle to meet the expectations placed upon them. Reports have been produced since the mid-1970s calling for reforms to be made. The Council of Ministers and the European Parliament have both funded enquiries into the state of the institutions and made recommendations. The European Parliament also produced a draft Union Treaty that specified the reforms it considered necessary. It is interesting to note the reforms called for and what actually appeared in the Single European Act and the Treaty on European Union, both of which amended the EC Treaty. The main omission was that although reforms associated with the European Commission were identified, they were not included. Apart from voting procedures in the Council and the "co-operation" and "co-decision" procedures, the main success was the setting up of the Court of First Instance to supplement the European Court of Justice. Why has there been this delay? It is often due to the individual perspective of the relationship between the institutions held by the governments of the Member States. After all it is these governments who must agree to such reforms in the Council of Ministers and obtain the ratification of the amendment in their national parliaments. The planned expansion in the number of Member States renewed the pressure for institutional reform and the Treaty of Amsterdam, but more importantly the Treaty of Nice, have brought about some reforms but not perhaps those thought necessary by some. However, at the Nice Inter-Governmental Conference (IGC) a declaration was made that has led to the establishment of the European Convention on the Future of Europe. This Convention has the remit to consider fundamental questions about the institutions needed by an enlarged EU. (See Chapter 11 TEU and Beyond, p.100).

"True Europeans"

Although the European Commissioners see themselves as the true Europeans as they have to take an independent European view on policy, the European Court see itself as having a very pro-European Community role. Perhaps the strongest example is the way the Court developed the principle of "Direct Effect" in the very early stages of the EC. It may also take the form of guarding its own position within the context of a unique international community as with the *Laying-up Fund* case in Opinion 1/76 or the recent *European Economic Area* case. Or recognising the exclusive Community competence, and thus European Commission role, in international negotiations in the *ERTA* case. The final example is the ECJ decisions allowing the European Parliament to bring an action under Art.230 EC (ex 173 EC) in certain circumstances, even though at that time the Parliament was not listed as a privileged applicant under the Article.

European Council

In 1974 the Heads of Government from the Member States began to meet to deal with some of the problems of political deadlock in the Council of Ministers. It was not formally recognised as an institution of the EC until Art.2 of the Single European Act stated that it should meet at least twice a year. Article 4 TEU states that "the European Council shall provide the Union with the necessary impetus for its development and shall define the general political guidelines thereof". Thus although it has no role in the formal legislative process of the Community, the European Council does play a very important part in deciding the future political direction of the Community.

2. SOURCES OF COMMUNITY LAW

PRIMARY AND SECONDARY SOURCES OF COMMUNITY LAW

The European Community is founded upon treaties. The transfer of sovereignty or powers from the Member States to the institutions of the Community is limited to specific policies and specific procedures to be found in the treaties. Thus the main treaties establishing the European Coal and Steel Community (ECSC), the European Community (but originally called the European Economic Community), EURATOM and most recently the Treaty on European Union (or Maastricht Treaty), as amended by the Treaties of Amsterdam and Nice, are the primary source of Community law. Wherever there is any doubt about the validity or authority of a particular measure, the lawyer should always go back to the source document, which invariably is one of the treaties. This is obviously in recognition of the international law aspect of the Community. All other sources of Community law are secondary or derived in that they originate from powers conferred on particular institutions by the treaties.

Treaties

The main treaties, listed above, set down the aims and objectives of the Community and provide a framework for legislation. The most important Treaty is the EC (previously the EEC), although the Treaty on European Union (TEU) has greatly extended the original Treaty of Rome signed in 1957 which formed the then European Economic Community. There are other treaties in the sense that there has to be one whenever new members join the Community, together with an Act of Accession for that particular member. In addition there have been important amendments to the original Treaty such as the Merger Treaty (1965) and the Single European Act or SEA (1986). However, these amend and do not replace the original Treaty.

Administrative Acts under Art.249 EC (ex 189 EC)

Article 249 EC (ex 189 EC) has been greatly amended by both the SEA and the TEU, principally to recognise the increasing role of the European Parliament. Under the Article "the European Parliament acting jointly with the Council, the Council and the Commission may, in order to carry out their tasks under the Treaty, make regulations, issue directives, take decisions, make recommendations or deliver opinions". Recommendations and opinions are not legally binding and therefore will not be considered in detail.

Regulations

Regulations are the most important derived source of Community law in that they are the chosen form when legislating for the whole Community, without going through any national channels. It is defined as "having general application, binding in its entirety and directly applicable in all member States". In the Joined Cases 16 & 17/62 *Producteurs de Fruits v Council* the Court stated that "a regulation, being essentially of a legislative nature, is applicable not to a limited number of persons, defined or identifiable, but to categories of persons viewed abstractly and in their entirety". The confusion over the term "directly applicable" is discussed with principle of direct effect in the next chapter (see p.30).

Directives

"Directives shall be binding, as to the result to be achieved, upon each Member State to which it is addressed, but shall leave to the national authorities the choice of form and methods".

This shows that directives lay down an objective and then leave it to the individual Member State to decide how best to achieve it. In the UK this may take the form of an Act of Parliament, as with the Consumer Protection Act 1987 or by one of the other methods available such as a statutory instrument. It may be that in a given situation, a Member State feels that it already has domestic legislation that meets most of the objectives set and will therefore merely introduce domestic legislation on the remainder. This does carry the hidden danger that they are mistaken and subsequent action in the national courts (Case 8/81 *Ursula Becker v Finanzamt*), or by the Commission under Art.226 EC (ex 169 EC) is necessary to enforce the obligation under the directive.

Although the form may differ between Member States, allowing for national traditions, the obligation on the Member State remains the same. Every directive specifies a time period, which is usually two years, by which time the Member State should have achieved the result required. If it has not done so, an individual may seek to enforce in their national courts any rights given to them under the directive by the principle of direct effect (Case 148/78 *Tullio Ratti v Ministero Pubblico*).

Decisions

Decisions are addressed to specific Member States, individuals or companies and are binding in their entirety upon those to whom they are addressed. They are most commonly used where the Commission has reached the conclusion that an undertaking is acting contrary to the competition policy of the Community under Art.81 or 82 EC (ex 85 or 86 EC).

Publication and Notification

Under Art.253 EC (ex 190 EC) regulations, directives and decisions must state the reasons on which they are based. In the preamble to such measures the justification or authority for them is based upon a Treaty article. They must be published in the Official Journal (Art.254 EC (ex 191 EC)). The regulation or directive of the Council and Commission will come into force on the date specified in them or if no date is given on the twentieth day following their publication. Decisions are notified to whom they are addressed and take effect upon notification.

All Community acts are numbered together with the year they were enacted. For example, a directive would appear as

Council Directive 64/221, recording that it was the 221 directive of 1964. Regulations have the year at the end, *i.e.* Council Regulation 4064/89.

Legislative Procedures under Art.249 EC (ex 189 EC)

There are different procedures which apply to different areas of legislation. The full list is given in Chapter 1 above (see p.3) but two procedures in particular require further discussion.

The Co-operation Procedure (Art.252 EC (ex 189c EC)) This procedure was introduced by the Single European Act 1986. The Commission proposal is sent to the European Parliament, which gives its opinion on the proposal. The proposal and the opinion of Parliament are then sent to the Council which adopts a "common position". The Council and the Commission inform the Parliament of the reasons for their respective positions. If, after three months the EP has approved the common position or not taken a decision, the Council can adopt the proposal in accordance with the common position. During the three months Parliament can propose amendments to the Council's common position or reject it outright, if approved by an absolute majority of its members. If the EP has rejected the position unanimity is required in the Council of Ministers if it is to adopt the proposal. The Commission has the power to withdraw or amend its proposal up until the time it has been adopted by the Council. Therefore, the Commission can re-examine the proposal in the light of any amendments of the European Parliament, although it has to give reasons for any it rejects. Lastly, the Council can adopt the Commission's final proposal by a qualified majority, although if it wishes to amend it unanimity is required.

Co-decision Procedure (Art.251 EC (ex 189b EC)) Although the term "co-decision" is not used in the Treaty, it is the popular name for this procedure introduced by the Treaty on European Union. The procedure has some of the elements of the Co-operation Procedure described above, but with the added ability of veto for the Parliament. Although the scope of the procedure is limited, it does apply to many of the areas which established the internal market and which may require amendment in the future. The scope of the procedure was reviewed in 1996 and in recognition of its success the areas of policy requiring the co-decision procedure to be used has been increased by both the Treaty of Amsterdam and the Treaty of Nice.

Under the Co-decision Procedure the Commission send a copy of their proposal to the Council and the European Parliament. The Parliament gives the proposal a "first reading". The Council then adopts a common position, giving its reasons for doing so to the European Parliament who then give the proposal a "second reading". At this stage the Parliament has three months in which to accept the Council's common position, in which case it is adopted by the Council as legislation or to reject it. If it does neither the Council's common position is accepted anyway. In the case of a rejection by an absolute majority of Parliament, a Conciliation Committee composed of equal number of representatives of the Council and Parliament is convened. The Commission also takes part in the work of this Committee, as it may alter its proposal at any time before it is adopted. The Committee has six weeks in which to approve a joint text, which if accepted by an absolute majority of Parliament and a qualified majority in the Council becomes adopted. Failure to agree such a joint text means that the proposal will fall unless within six weeks a qualified majority of the Council confirm their common position, in which case it will be adopted. Even in these circumstances the proposal can still be defeated if within six weeks the Parliament rejects the text of the common position by an absolute majority of its members. The periods of three months and six weeks referred to above can be extended by a maximum of one month and two weeks respectively by agreement by the Council and the Parliament.

GENERAL PRINCIPLES OF COMMUNITY LAW

These are an important source of Community law in that they provide a useful tool for interpretation and allow Community law to be challenged on the basis that it is contrary to a general principle of Community law. They may also support a claim for damages under Art.288 EC (ex 215(2) EC). Every legal jurisdiction has its own general principles, which are principles which command common assent, such as the right to natural justice. The ECJ has justified its action by referring to three articles in the Treaty. Article 220 EC (ex 164 EC) states that the Court shall ensure that in the interpretation and application of the Treaty the law is observed. Secondly in Art.230 EC (ex 173 EC) the grounds for annulment include "infringement of the Treaty, or of any rule of law relating to its application". In both of these references "law" must refer to something outside the Treaty itself. Lastly, Art.288(2) EC (ex 215(2) EC), which is concerned with non-contractual liability, expressly provides that the liability of the Community is based on the "general principles common to the laws of the Member States".

The ECJ has derived general principles of Community law from the Treaties and from the legal systems of the Member States. For example, Art.7 EC (now repealed) which prohibited discrimination based on nationality was used by the ECJ as the foundation for a general principle which forbids arbitrary discrimination on any ground. Article 6 TEU contains a strong statement in relation to fundamental rights of citizens of the EU. When looking at the legal systems of the Member States the ECJ is not looking for a principle to be common to all of them before it may be adopted. It is sufficient if it is generally accepted. Whatever the factual origin of the principle, it is applied by the ECJ as a general principle of Community law. The most important examples of general principles are:

Proportionality

A public authority may not impose obligations on a citizen except to the extent to which they are strictly necessary in the public interest to attain the purpose of the measure. If the burdens imposed are clearly out of proportion to the object in view, the measure will be annulled if challenged in the courts. This principle, derived from German law, is important in economic law where levies or charges are involved. In the *Skimmed-Milk Powder* case (Case 114/76) the Commission needed to reduce a surplus of skimmed-milk powder in the Community by requiring animal feed producers to incorporate it into their products in place of soya. Unfortunately this also meant that the price of the feed would be increased by three fold. The ECJ declared the regulation concerned was invalid, partly because it discriminated against some farmers and partly because it was against the principle of proportionality. The requirement placed on the producers was not necessary in order to diminish the surplus.

Protection of Legitimate Expectations

This is another principle derived from German law, whereby Community measures must not violate the legitimate expectations of those concerned, unless there is an overriding matter of public interest. In Case 78/74 *Deuka v EVGF*, the ECJ interpreted a Commission regulation setting the denaturing premiums for common wheat so as to protect the legitimate expectations of the processors.

Non-discrimination

As was mentioned above this was derived from the Treaty Arts 7 (now repealed) and 141 EC (ex 119 EC). However, the ECJ has gone beyond these specific provisions to hold that there is a general principle of non-discrimination (see *Deuka v EVGF* above). In Case 20/71 *Sabbatini v European Parliament* Sabbatini, who was employed by the European Parliament, successfully used the principle against her employer's staff regulations when she lost an expatriation allowance on her marriage. In Case 130/75 *Prais v Council* the principle was extended to discrimination on the grounds of religion.

Protection of Fundamental Rights

In Case 29/69 *Stauder v Ulm* the ECJ recognised that the protection of such rights was inspired by the constitutional traditions common to all the Member States. The protection of fundamental rights was therefore enshrined in the general principles of Community law and thus protected by the ECJ. Stauder had been required to give his name when he applied for cheap butter under a Community scheme. Case 11/70 *Internationale Handelsgesellschaft* took the recognition of this principle a step further as the German courts were unhappy with the Community's protection of fundamental rights in contrast with that provided by the German Basic law. (See also Case 44/79 *Hauer v Land Rheinland-Pfalz*). There was a similar discussion in Italy in Case 33/84 *Fragd v Amministrazione delle Finanze dello Stato*. Article 6 TEU now gives specific recognition of this general principle. There is a Charter of Fundamental Rights of the EU but this is not legally binding, although it is likely that the Court will draw on its provisions when considering fundamental rights. The 2004 IGC is to consider whether the Charter should have the force of law.

Procedural Rights

The main procedural rights are the right to be heard and the right to due process.

(a) Right to be Heard   Based on English law this principle requires that a person whose interests are perceptively affected by a decision taken by a public authority must be given the opportunity to make his point of view known (Case 17/74 *Transocean Marine Paint v Commission*).

(b) Right to Due Process   This right follows on from the duty of those exercising authority to give reasons for a decision. In Case 222/84 *Johnston v Chief Constable of the Royal Ulster Constabulary* a certificate issued by the Secretary of State for Northern Ireland sought to provide exclusive evidence that the derogation from Community obligations under Directive 76/207 was on the grounds of national security. Mrs Johnston claimed that she had been subject to sex discrimination by her employer, contrary to Community law. The ECJ held that the action of the Secretary of State was contrary to the requirement of judicial control, recognised as a general principle by the Member States.

JUDGMENTS OF THE EUROPEAN COURT OF JUSTICE AND THE COURT OF FIRST INSTANCE

Although these courts do not follow the system of binding precedent found in common law jurisdictions such as England, they do accept the importance of certainty as a principle of law. Therefore the judgments of previous cases before these courts do affect future cases. After all the ECJ is the final arbiter of Community law. They are thus a source of Community law when an individual is seeking to identify what the law is. For example, there have been certain cases which appear to have no obvious connection with either the Treaty or legislative act, but which have been used by the Court of Justice to develop the principle of direct effect.

Methods of Interpretation

When called upon to identify what the law is the ECJ has to interpret the treaties, administrative acts and other *sui generis* sources of law. To assist in this process the ECJ has evolved a number of methods of interpretation, which other courts can utilise when dealing with questions of Community law. The methods used by the ECJ have been influenced by the traditions of the Member States, notably France and Germany. However, there are special problems facing the Court, including the linguistic one that there are nine official versions of a text. This principle of linguistic equality has affected the Court as it has developed a particular "Community way" of interpretation. The main "tools" of interpretation used by the Court are:

(a) teleological, which requires the judge to look to the purpose or object of the text before him;

(b) the contextual approach, which involves the court placing the provision within its context and interpreting it in relation to other provisions of Community law;

(c) historical interpretation requires an attempt to ascertain the subjective intention of the author by looking at documentation available to the court;

(d) literal interpretation is familiar to any judge, but with Community law once its literal meaning has been identified it is then necessary to apply the teleological or contextual approach.

The Court appears to favour the first two methods of interpretation, teleological and contextual, as they assist in the development of the Community towards the objectives listed in the first part of the EC Treaty.

3. EC & NATIONAL LAW

SUPREMACY OF COMMUNITY LAW

The relationship between Community and national law was established in one of the earliest cases to come before the European Court of Justice. In Case 6/64 *Costa v ENEL* an action was brought in Italy against the nationalised National Electricity Board (ENEL) over a bill of 1,950 lire which then amounted to less than £1. Mr Costa claimed that he was not obliged to pay the bill as the nationalisation legislation had infringed Italian and EC law. A reference was made by the Italian court under Art.234 EC (ex 177 EC). The Italian government argued that such a reference was "absolutely inadmissible" because the national court had to apply national law.

The ECJ rejected that argument in a passage which has been repeated on many subsequent occasions.

> "By contrast with ordinary international treaties, the EEC Treaty has created its own legal system which . . . became an integral part of the legal systems of the Member States and which their courts are bound to apply. By creating a Community of unlimited duration, having its own institutions, its own personality, its own legal capacity . . . and real powers stemming from a limitation of sovereignty or a transfer of powers from the States to the Community, the Member States have limited their sovereign rights, albeit within limited fields, and thus created a body of law which binds both their nationals and themselves . . . It follows . . . that the law stemming from the Treaty, an independent source of law, could not, because of its special and original nature, be overridden by domestic legal provisions, however framed, without being deprived of its character as Community law and without the legal basis of the Community itself being called into question."

Community Law Prevails

Thus on the basis of a case involving very little money the principle was established that where there is conflict between Community law and national law it is Community law which is to prevail. If it was otherwise "the obligations under the Treaty could be called into question" by any subsequent national legislation the government of a Member State passed through its legislature. *Costa v ENEL* developed this basic principle which had been set down in Case 26/62 *Van Gend en Loos v Nederlanse Tarief commissie* one year earlier.

Although the Treaties do not expressly mention the principle of supremacy, a number of provisions require it. For the ECJ the position is unequivocal. By creating the Community the Member States consented to transfer to it certain of their powers and to restrict their sovereign rights. The ECJ case-law is directed at the national courts who apply the law in the cases which come before them and apply effective remedies. Thus we have the statement in Case 92/78 *Simmenthal v Commission* that the provisions of Community law "are an integral part of, and take precedence in, the legal order applicable in the territory of each of the Member States".

Full recognition was given to the principle of supremacy in Case 221/89 *R. v Secretary of State for Transport, Ex p. Factortame Ltd* where Lord Bridge in the House of Lords stated: "If the supremacy within the EC of Community law over the national law of the Member States was not always inherent in the EEC Treaty it was certainly well established in the jurisprudence of the Court of Justice long before the UK joined the Community. Thus, whatever limitation of its sovereignty Parliament accepted when it enacted the European Communities Act 1972 was entirely voluntary". Therefore, Community law will prevail over inconsistent UK legislation, even where that legislation has been enacted by Parliament subsequent to the entry into force of the Community rule. In *Equal Opportunities Commission v Secretary of State for Employment* [1995] 1 A.C. 1 the House of Lords held that the Employment Protection (Consolidation) Act 1978 requirements regarding qualifying periods of employment were contrary to European law.

Incorporation of Community law into National law

When a State joins the European Community it is obliged to reconcile its constitution with Community membership. It does this by making provision for the application of Community law within its territory and for the supremacy of Community law over national law. How the State will achieve this will depend upon its conception of international law as there are two possibilities, namely monist and dualist.

Monist Approach The monist conception is that international law and national law are both part of one legal structure, even though they operate in different spheres. In such countries there is no reason why the national courts should not apply international law, provided that the appropriate constitutional procedures have been gone through to receive them into the national system. In cases where there is a conflict with national law, monist countries usually recognise the supremacy of treaty provisions, as for example happens in France and the Netherlands.

Dualist Approach The dualist conception is that international law and national law are two fundamentally different structures. Therefore in such countries international treaties as such can never be applied by national courts unless domestic legislation makes this possible. The UK is a dualist country and therefore the European Communities Act 1972 was specifically enacted to make provision for UK membership of the Community. Lord Denning made clear in *McWhirter v Att-Gen* [1972] C.M.L.R. 882 that without this Act the EC Treaty and Community legislation would have been binding on the UK in international law but would have had no effect internally. Sections 2 and 3 of the European Communities Act 1972 achieve this purpose.

DIRECT EFFECT

This important principle was created by the ECJ and follows on from the principle of supremacy of Community law. It is a novel concept and can appear complex in the way it applies to particular Community provisions. If a legal provision is said to be directly effective, it means that it grants individual rights that must be upheld by the national courts. There are two initial requirements that have to be satisfied as the provision must be part of the legal order and its terms must be appropriate to confer rights on individuals. There is thus a close link between supremacy of Community law and direct effect as they both flow from the nature of the Community. In the important case of Case 26/62 *Van Gend en Loos v Nederlanse Tariefcommissie*, Van Gend imported chemicals from Germany. In 1959 a Dutch law was passed which imposed a duty on some imported chemicals. This was contrary to Art.25 EC (ex 12 EC) which required Member States to refrain from introducing new duties or raising existing ones on imports between the States. Van Gend objected to paying the duty and a reference was made under Art.234 EC (ex 177 EC) to the ECJ to ascertain whether the duty on the chemicals was prohibited.

The conclusion reached by the ECJ was that

> "the Community constitutes a new legal order of international law for the benefit of which the states have limited their sovereign rights, albeit within limited fields, and the subject of which comprise not only the Member States but also their nationals. Independently of the legislation of the Member States, Community law therefore not only imposes obligations on individuals but is also intended to confer upon them rights which become part of their legal heritage".

Direct Effect and Member States

The judgment in *Van Gend* was not the one which the Member States argued for. As far as they were concerned if there was a breach of a Community obligation the Treaty provided for action to be taken by the Commission under Art.226 EC (ex 169 EC), or by another Member State under Art.227 EC (ex 170 EC) These procedures have the advantage for the Member State that they take a long time to come before the ECJ and, until the Maastricht Treaty, did not carry any real sanction. The statements in *Van Gend*, clearly giving the individual who is affected by Community law the equipment to take action in his national courts, ensure that the Member States observe their obligations.

Conditions for Direct Effect

The principle of direct effect is a very powerful one and the ECJ has taken the view that it has to be limited by being interpreted restrictively. The judgment in *Van Gend* pointed out that Art.25 EC (ex 12 EC) was ideally adapted to have direct effect on the legal relations between the Member States and their subjects. The Court did this by establishing what are now recognised as the conditions which must apply if direct effect is to be enforced. These are:

1. The provision must be clear and unambiguous;
2. It must be unconditional; and
3. Its operation must not be dependent on further action being taken by Community or national authorities.

The principle of direct effect has been applied to all the legally binding sources of Community law. Whether or not a provision has direct effect is a question of interpretation of Community law. In this way the ECJ seeks to ensure uniformity throughout the Community.

Direct Effect of Treaty Provisions

The ECJ established in *Van Gend en Loos* that Treaty articles which impose on Member States an obligation to abstain from something, such as levying duties under Art.25 EC (ex 12C EC), have direct effect. In Case 57/67 *Firma Alfons Lutticke GmbH v Hauptzollamt* a preliminary reference was made asking if Art.90 EC (ex 95 EC), which deals with taxation, had direct effect. The Court used the familiar phrases when it stated, "The first paragraph of Article 90 EC (ex 95EC) contains a prohibition against discrimination, constituting a clear and unconditional obligation". There being no discretion left to Member States, it concluded that Art.90 EC (ex 95 EC) produced direct effects and creates individual rights of which national courts must take account. See also Case 43/75 *Defrenne v Sabena (No. 2)*.

Direct Effect of Regulations

Under Art.249 EC (ex 189 EC) Regulations have general application and are binding in their entirety and directly applicable in all Member States. The term used in the article is "directly applicable" and not "direct effect", although as the ECJ often use the terms inconsistently there is often confusion as to the difference in meaning. Direct applicability is not the same as direct effect, as the conditions or test mentioned above still has to be satisfied if direct effect is to be applied. Direct applicability means that the national courts must apply a regulation whenever their contents grants rights to individuals or impose obligations on them. In the *Politi* judgment (Case 43/71 *Politi v Ministry for Finance of the Italian Republic*) the Court held that "by reason of their nature and their function in the system of the sources of Community law, regulations have direct effect and are, as such, capable of creating individual rights which national courts must protect". The resulting enforcement of his rights by the individual are the same whether the regulation is said to be directly applicable or directly effective.

In Case 93/71 *Orsolina Leonesio v Ministero dell'agricoltura e foreste* an Italian farmer claimed a subsidy for slaughtering a cow under Community regulations. The Italian government refused on the basis that under the Italian Constitution national legislation had to be enacted before they could do so. The ECJ held that regulations become part of the national legal system and the direct applicability under Art.249 EC (ex 189 EC) cannot be hindered by national practices. There are instances where regulations do require further legislation, such as in the form of directives. In these circumstances the condition that the provision must not be dependent on further action being taken cannot be satisfied.

Direct Effect of Decisions

In Case 9/70 *Franz Grad v Finanzamt Traunstein* the ECJ held that Decisions could have vertical direct effect:

> "the provisions according to which decisions are binding in their entirety on those to whom they are addressed enables the question

to be put whether the obligation created by the decisions can only be invoked by the Community institutions against the addressee or whether such a right may possibly be exercised by all those who have an interest in the fulfilment of this obligation".

The answer given by the Court was that all those with an interest should have the right.

Direct Effect of Directives

In contrast to the direct applicability of regulations, Art.249 EC (ex 189 EC) states that directives are addressed to Member States and are binding as to the result to be achieved. The Member States have argued that this wording means that directives cannot be directly effective because they cannot satisfy the conditions. This view was supported by the Conseil d'Etat in *Minister of the Interior v Cohn-Bendit* [1980] 1 C.M.L.R. 543. If the choice is left to the Member States as to the form and method to achieve the obligation, they must require further action in the form of domestic legislation required. The ECJ has not accepted this argument. The effectiveness (*l'effet utile*) of a directive would be weakened if the nationals of a Member State which had failed to implement or had implemented it wrongly were denied by the national court the rights contained in the directive. This was stated in *Grad* which although concerned with a Community Decision developed the principle which was closer repeated in Case 41/74 *Yvonne Van Duyn v Home Office* which did involve a directive. (See now Case 91/92 *Paola Faccini Dori v Recreb Srl*).

The Principle   In *Van Duyn* it was Directive 64/221 concerning restriction on the admission and movement of aliens which required interpretation. Miss Van Duyn, a Dutch national sought a declaration that the UK government was wrong to deny her admission to take up employment with the Church of Scientology, a sect which the government considered undesirable. On a preliminary reference under Art.234 EC (ex 177 EC), the ECJ held that the Directive was directly effective because it "imposes on a Member State a precise obligation which does not require the adoption of any further measure on the part of either the Community institutions or of the member States and which leaves them, in relation to its implementation, no discretionary powers". Thus the conditions for direct effect were satisfied, although on the facts of the case it agreed that the UK government could exclude her.

In Case 148/78 *Criminal proceedings against Tullio Ratti* the ECJ took the opportunity to refine its arguments for direct effect of directives. "A Member State which has not adopted the implementing measures required by a directive in the prescribed period may not rely, as against individuals, on it own failure to perform the obligations which the directive entails". If it was the government which had not fulfilled its obligations arising from the Directive, it is against the government that rights arising from the Directive can be enforced. In Case 81/83 *Ursula Becker v Finanzamt Munster-Innenstadt,* a German credit broker successfully claimed the benefit of a provision of the sixth VAT Directive against the German VAT authorities as they had failed to implement the Directive. In the important case of Case 271/91 *Marshall v Southampton and South West Hampshire AHA* the UK government had failed to properly implement the Equal Treatment Directive 76/207, which was held to be directly effective.

Vertical and Horizontal Direct Effect

Both articles of the Treaty and regulations have been held by the ECJ as being capable of giving both horizontal and vertical direct effect. Vertical effect means that an individual can invoke the obligation arising from the provision against the Member State before a national court. Horizontal effect means that an individual can invoke the obligation arising from the provision against another individual before the national court. It was also made clear in the *Marshall* judgment that there was no question of a directive having horizontal direct effect.

Mrs Marshall was employed by the Southampton Area Health Authority when she was dismissed because she had reached the age of 62, the Authority's retirement age for females. The ECJ accepted that this was contrary to Equal Treatment Directive 76/207. As the Area Health Authority was an "emanation of the State", Mrs Marshall succeeded in her action. This is also illustrated by Case 188/89 *Foster v British Gas* where the employer was the pre-privatised Gas Board. In contrast Mrs Duke who was employed by a public company, GEC Reliance Ltd, did not succeed because she was requesting horizontal effect to enforce the Directive against another individual, albeit a company. The principle is therefore, that unless the individual is able to show that there is some relationship with the State the principle of direct effect will not apply even if all three conditions mentioned above can be fulfilled. (See *Webb v EMO Cargo Ltd* [1993] 1 W.L.R. 49).

In a number of cases Advocate-Generals have called on the Court to abolish the distinction between vertical and horizontal direct effect of directives. In Case 91/92 *Faccini Dori v Recreb Srl* (1995) the ECJ refused to follow this path. In this case the Court found that the relevant provisions of the directive were unconditional and sufficiently precise, but stated that if the Community wished to enact obligations between individuals with immediate effect it could do so by adopting regulations.

Every Directive involves a time-scale for implementation. This period, normally two years, is to give the government of the Member State time to formulate and pass the appropriate domestic measure. Until this period has elapsed the Directive cannot, as was confirmed in *Ratti*, have direct effect. Ratti ran a business in Italy selling solvents and varnishes. The Community had adopted two Directives specifying the labelling and packaging of these products. Italy had not implemented the Directives but Ratti had complied with them with regard to his products. Unfortunately for him the domestic legislation in Italy set other requirements which he had breached and was prosecuted before the Italian court. A preliminary reference was made to the ECJ which held that as the time for the implementation of one of the Directives had passed it was directly effective thus providing Ratti with a defence. The other Directive still had time to be implemented and therefore could not be directly effective until that time had expired.

In Case 208/90 *Emmott v Minister for Social Welfare*, Mrs Emmott brought an action against the Irish Minister for Social Welfare on the basis that she received less benefit than a man would have done in equivalent circumstances. Directive 79/7 should have been implemented by 1984 but was not implemented in Ireland until 1988. Mrs Emmott's action in 1987 followed a previous case before the ECJ where it had declared that the Directive had direct effect. The verticle relationship between herself and the Irish government satisfied the case law of the Court. The Irish government, however, claimed that her action was statute barred because it had not been brought within the three months required by Irish law for judicial review. The Court held that Community law precludes the competent national authorities from relying on national procedural rules relating to time limits to stop an action by one of its citizens seeking to enforce a right that Member State has failed to transpose into its domestic legal system. The time limit does not run until the date when the national implementing legislation is correctly adopted.

Von Colson Principle

If a Community act cannot satisfy the three conditions for direct effect, the individual cannot seek to have any right arising from it enforced in the national courts. This is what happened in the _Von Colson_ and _Harz_ cases (Case 14/83 _Von Colson and Kamann v Land Nordrhein-Westfalen_ and Case 79/83 _Harz v Deutsche Tradax GmbH_ when women sought remedies in the German courts for unlawful discrimination. They claimed that this was contrary to the Equal Treatment Directive 1976. On a preliminary reference the ECJ was asked whether Art.6 of the Directive had direct effect. The Court did not restrict itself to the question whether there was vertical or horizontal direct effect. Instead it used Art.5 EC which requires Member States to "take all appropriate measures to ensure fulfilment of their Community obligations". Therefore even if the principle of direct effect does not apply, the courts in the Member States are required to interpret national legislation specifically passed to implement the Community act to comply with Community law.

In _Litster v Forth Dry Dock & Engineering Co Ltd_ [1990] 1 A.C. 546, the House of Lords interpreted the Transfer of Undertakings (Protection of Employment) Regulation 1981 in such a way as to give effect to the Directive 77/187. This was because it was for the purpose of implementing the Directive that the domestic Regulation had been introduced. In this way the House of Lords was using the _Von Colson_ principle to give effect not only to the Directive but also the subsequent interpretation by the ECJ of the Directive in Case 101/87 _Bork International v Forening af Arbejdsledere I Danmark_.

In Case 106/89 _Marleasing SA v La Comercial Internacional de Alimentacion SA_, the _Von Colson_ principle was taken a stage further when the ECJ held that the principle could be applied even if the necessary national legislation had not been introduced to comply with the Directive. However, the ECJ has limited the _Von Colson_ principle with regard to criminal prosecutions, if this would make the accused guilty where he would otherwise have been acquitted. (See Case 80/86 _Officer van Justitie v Koplinghuis Nijmegen_ and Case 168/95 _Criminal proceedings against Luciano Arcaro_).

Direct Effect and Claims for Damages

In Case 479/93 *Francovich v Italian State* the ECJ extended the impact of the law regarding directives. "Community law lays down a principle according to which a Member State is liable to make good damage to individuals caused by a breach of Community law for which it is responsible". Under a Council Directive aimed at protecting employees in the event of the insolvency of their employers', Member States were required to ensure that payment of employees' outstanding claims arising from the employment relationship and relating to pay was guaranteed. Unfortunately the Italian government had not set up any Italian system to act as a guarantor in these circumstances, hence his claim against them. Mr Francovich was owed 6 million lire by his insolvent employers. As he was unable to enforce a judgment against them, he brought an action against the Italian government for compensation. The ECJ held that damages are available against the State for failure to implement EC directives, if three conditions are met. The conditions are:

1. that the result required by the directive includes the conferring of rights for the benefit of individuals;
2. the content of those rights is identifiable by reference to the directive, and
3. there exists a causal link between the breach of the State's obligations and the damage suffered by the person affected.

Limits for damages Case 271/91 *Marshall v Southampton and South West Hampshire AHA* followed a successful action by Mrs Marshall against her employer under the Equal Treatment Directive. Under UK enacting legislation there was a limit imposed on the compensation payable for sex discrimination and no interest was allowed on this sum. The ECJ in this second case rejected the UK government's argument that limits on compensation were matters for national law. Article 6 of the Directive was directly effective and therefore such compensation had to be "adequate" to make good the loss sustained by the individual as a result of the wrongful discrimination. In computing the amount of compensation, interest should be included from the date of the discrimination.

In Cases 46/93 and 48/93 *Brasserie du Pecheur and Factortame (No 4)* judgment the ECJ stated that the principles in *Francovich* applied whether it was an act or omission by the organ of the state which caused the breach. If the three conditions were met the national court could award exemplary damages if such damages could be awarded in similar claims founded on domestic law. National legislation which generally limited the damage for which reparation could be granted was not compatible with Community Law. The three conditions are

  (i) the rule of law infringed must be intended to confer rights on individuals,
 (ii) the breach must be sufficiently serious and
(iii) there must be a causal link between the breach of the obligation resting on the state and the damage sustained by the injured parties.

These three conditions are a development of these stated in *Francovich*. The decisive test for finding that a breach of community law was sufficiently serious was whether the member state or the Community institution had manifestly and gravely disregarded the limits on its discretion. (See Lord Bingham's judgment in *R. v Secretary of State for the Home Department, Ex p. Gallagher* [1996] 2 C.M.L.R. 951).

4. Preliminary References

Under the system of preliminary references a court in any Member State may make a reference to the ECJ in order to ascertain its view with regard to the interpretation or validity. The case in the Member States is suspended while the question(s) are despatched for consideration by the ECJ. When the Court has given its judgment the answers are sent back to the national courts which, having had the Community law clarified for them, apply it to the case before them in the normal way. The period that it takes for this process to take place is around 18 months, although every effort is made by the ECJ to reduce this timescale.

Objectives of Preliminary References

As was shown in Chapter 3 above, p.27 the principle was established whereby Community law must override national law in the event of a conflict. To do otherwise would allow a Member State to avoid the application of Community law which they considered disadvantageous by the simple expedient of passing conflicting legislation for their national courts to apply. As Community law does have this superiority over national law it is important that such law should have the same meaning and effect in all Member States. This requires that there should be a single court, the ECJ, whose jurisdiction extends over the whole Community. Also if Community law is under certain circumstances to be directly effective, the ECJ must have the final say with regard to its validity and interpretation. Thus the objectives of the preliminary reference procedure under Art.234 EC (ex 177 EC) is to provide for a definitive judgment regarding the interpretation and validity of Community law.

Matters for Referral under Art.234(1) EC (ex 177(1) EC)

Although there are three parts to this subsection of Art.234 EC (ex 177 EC), it is the first two which are the most important. These are the ability to give preliminary rulings on:

(a) the interpretation of the Treaty; and
(b) the validity and interpretation of acts of the institutions and of the ECB.

There is an obvious distinction in that there is only the possibility of seeking interpretation of the Treaty as its validity cannot be challenged. This is what one would expect when the Treaty is seen as the primary source of Community law. The "acts of the institutions" refers to the European Parliament, Council and Commission making legally binding acts defined in Art.249 EC (ex 189 EC) such as Regulations and Directives. The European Central Bank (ECB) was added by the Treaty on European Union.

Direct Effect and 234 EC References There are two important points to make which show that the list above is not exhaustive. Firstly, as was shown in the last chapter, the principle of direct effect has had an important influence on the development of Community law. The ECJ has used the procedure for preliminary rulings to look at the effectiveness of Community provisions, as well as the supremacy of Community law. The majority of the most important cases on Community law have only been brought before the Court by the Art.234 EC (ex 177 EC) procedure. Although the Court would argue that it is merely exercising its authority as interpreter of Community law, it is in reality going much further than what would normally be regarded as interpretation.

The result is that there are really three issues which may be referred to the Court for a ruling; interpretation, effect and, for certain provisions, validity. Questions of fact and of national law may not be referred, nor may the Court rule on the application of the law to the particular facts of the case. However, the boundary between interpretation and application is sometime uncertain and although the ECJ may cross it the national court receiving the ruling can decide for itself.

The second point is that wherever possible the Court has taken a liberal view with regard to the "acts" of the institutions it is called upon to consider. It is not restricted to Art.249 EC (ex 189 EC). For example, although agreements with non-Member States are clearly not part of the Treaty they are negotiated by the Commission and concluded by the Council under procedures and powers to be found in Art.300 EC (ex 228 EC) of the Treaty. Thus in Case 181/73 *R & V Haegeman v Belgium* the Court seized upon this ground for regarding the Association Agreement between the Community and Greece as a Community act and therefore covered by Art.234(1)(b) EC (ex 177(1)(b) EC). Having done this the Court then went on to interpret the Agreement itself! The view of the Court is that since such international agreements are part of Community law and binding on the Member States, it is clearly desirable that they should receive uniform interpretation throughout the Community. Obviously the ruling of the Court is not binding on the other party, *i.e.* Greece in the *Haegeman* case as they were not members of the Community at that time.

General principles of Community law may not form the subject matter of a reference as they are neither part of the Treaty nor are they Community acts. However, as was illustrated above, the Art.234 EC (ex 177 EC) procedure has been used with regard to them by the simple expedient of using a suitable Treaty provision or Community act to provide a beg on which to hang the general principle. The latter can then be interpreted in the course of the reference.

Which Courts are Covered by Art.234 EC (ex 177 EC)?

Article 234(2) and 234(3) EC (ex 177(2) and 177(3) EC) both refer to courts and tribunals. There are two requirements that these must fulfil. Firstly, the body requesting the reference must be a court or tribunal and, secondly they must be of a Member State. This second requirement is straightforward but the first has produced some clear statements from the Court.

Court or Tribunal? For the ECJ it does not matter what the body is called or whether it is recognised as a court or tribunal under national law. The key question of the Court is whether it performs a judicial function. What constitutes a "judicial function" is not always easy to clarify, but generally a body is regarded as judicial if it has power to give binding determinations of the legal rights and obligations of individuals. In Case 61/65 *Vaassen v Beamtenfonds Mijnbedrij* a reference was made by an "arbitration tribunal", which settled disputes regarding the pension fund for the Dutch mining industry. The fund had been set up privately with representatives of both employers and employees and was approved by the ministers responsible for both the mines and social security. Members of the tribunal were appointed by the minister and any pension dispute had to go before it and be subject to its adversary procedure. The Court of Justice concluded that this tribunal came within Art.234 EC (ex 177 EC) because it was a judicial body representing the power of the State and settling as a matter of law disputes concerning the application of the pension scheme. In contrast, the ECJ refused to give a ruling in Case 138/80 *Borker, Re* on a reference from the Paris Chambre des Avocats on the ground that it was not exercising a judicial function. In Cases 69/96–79/96 *Garofalo v Ministers della Sanita* the ECJ specified a number of factors to be taken into account in order to determine whether a body is a "court or tribunal".

The conclusion from this is that all administrative tribunals established in the UK by statute would be recognised as having a right under Art.234 EC (ex 177 EC) to make a reference. However, if they were merely domestic tribunals the ECJ would have to decide whether the element of acting for the state, the adversarial procedure and possible recourse to the national courts were sufficient for it to be within the Art.234 EC (ex 177 EC) procedure.

Preliminary References and National Law

Where a court or tribunal has a right to make a reference under Art.234 EC (ex 177 EC), it cannot be deprived of that right by national law. The Court stated this rule in the *Rheinmuhlen* cases which were heard in the German Tax Courts. The lower court hearing the case wished to make a reference to the ECJ as a number of questions had been raised which required interpretation. This was despite a ruling having been given to it by the higher Federal Tax Court. In the end both German courts made a reference. The Federal Tax Court asked whether Art.234 EC (ex 177 EC) gives lower courts an unfettered right to refer, or whether it is subject to national provisions under which lower courts are bound by the judgments of superior courts. The response of the ECJ was unequivocal. The power of a lower court to make a reference cannot be abrogated by a provision of national law. Lower courts must be free to make a reference if it considers that the superior court's ruling could lead it to give judgment contrary to Community law. (See Chadwick L.J. in *Trent Taverns Ltd v Sykes* [1999] Eu.L.R. 492).

The practical situation is that national law cannot take away the right given by Art.234(2) EC (ex 177(2) EC), but this does not prevent the lower court's order for a reference being quashed on appeal. In *R. v Plymouth Justices, Ex p. Rogers* [1982] Q.B. 863, Lord Lane C.J. stated that magistrates had the jurisdiction to make a reference but that they should consider whether a higher court might be in a better position to assess the need for a reference and to formulate the questions to be sent to the Court. A counter argument has been put in that if a reference seems likely to be made at some stage in the proceedings, time may actually be saved if this is done as soon as possible, for an appeal within the domestic system may thereby be obviated.

Article 234(2) EC (ex 177(2) EC)

The word "may" appears in this Article, giving those courts and tribunals concerned a discretion as to whether or not to make a reference to the ECJ. There are two requisites which have to be fulfilled before Art.234(2) (ex 177(2) EC) comes into operation.

1. An appropriate question of Community law must be raised before the court. In fact the "question" can be raised by either the parties to the action or the court itself, as is allowed for under the procedural rules in England (RSC Order 114 r.2(1)).
2. A decision on that question must be necessary to enable the court to give judgment. It should be noted that it is not the reference which is necessary but a decision on the

question. The Treaty makes it clear that this is for the national court to decide and the ECJ will not question the necessity of the decision or whether Community law is even applicable to the case. Lord Denning in *Bulmer v Bollinger* [1974] 3 W.L.R 202 said that "necessary" meant that the outcome of the case must be dependent on the decision. "If the Community point is decided one way, judgment for one party must be the result; if it decided in another way, judgment must be given for the other party". This is perhaps too restrictive an interpretation. A better suggestion is that "necessary" should be interpreted to mean that the point could be decisive. To assist in this process it is better if the facts of the case are fully ascertained before a reference is made. This will help because it may result in the national court deciding that the case can be settled on a point of national law and a reference would not be required. However, it should be remembered that under RSC Order 114 a reference may be made at any stage in the proceedings. In Case 157/92 *Pretore di Genova v Banchero* the ECJ said that the national court must define the factual and legal framework in which the questions arise before making a preliminary reference.

Previous Judgments of the ECJ to Preliminary References

It may be that the question for interpretation or validity specified in Art.234(1) EC (ex 177(1) EC) has already come before the ECJ and it has provided an answer. In such circumstances the point may be regarded as settled and the authority of the previous ruling would remove the need to make a reference. However, it should be remembered that the ECJ does not have the same judicial tradition towards precedent as English courts, and that if the national court wishes to exercise the right under Art.234 EC (ex 177 EC) it cannot be fettered.

Article 234(3) (ex 177(3) EC)

This Article appears to lay down an obligation to make a reference where the court or tribunal of a Member State is one "against whose decision there is no judicial remedy under national law". What courts are included? There are two propositions, an Abstract Theory and a Concrete Theory.

Abstract Theory

Only those courts whose decisions are never subject to appeal are within the scope of this provision. For example in the UK the House of Lords would obviously be the only court in this category.

Concrete Theory

The important question is whether the court's decision in the case in question is subject to appeal. An example of this would be the case of *Costa v ENEL*, where the sum involved in the case meant that there could be no appeal from the lower court within the Italian court system.

The literal reading of the Art.234(3) EC (ex 177(3) EC) would seem to favour the Abstract Theory. Certainly Lord Denning was of the opinion in *Bulmer v Bollinger* that only the House of Lords came with the scope of this Article. However, the ECJ appears to favour the Concrete Theory when it suggests that Art.234(3) (ex 177(3) EC) refers to the highest court in the case rather than the highest court in the Member State (*Costa v ENEL*). The case of *Chiron Corp v Murex Diagnostics* [1994] F.S.R. 202 discussed these issues in relation to the Court of Appeal and the House of Lords.

Obligation to Refer

As early as Case 28/62 *Da Costa en Schaake v Netherlands Inland Revenue Administration* the ECJ had stated that if the Court had already pronounced on a question of interpretation it might deprive the obligation to refer of its purpose and empty it of its substance. The important ECJ judgment in Case 283/81 *CILFIT v Ministry of Health* put the obligation on Art.234(3) EC (ex 177(3) EC) courts to make a reference in a clearer position. In this case the Court said that the obligation to refer was based on co-operation between the national courts and the ECJ. The purpose of this co-operation was to prevent divergencies in judicial decisions on question of Community law, *i.e.* uniformity. It may be that the correct application of Community law was so obvious that there was no scope for reasonable doubt about the answers to any questions raised. This reflects the principle of *acte clair*.

Acte Clair

This principle has its origins in French law, where the ordinary courts were required to request a ruling from the Ministry of

Foreign Affairs on a question of treaty interpretation unless the point was regarded as clear. Thus in relation to preliminary references under Art.234(3) EC (ex 177(3) EC) the courts might consider that the state of Community law is sufficiently clear to be applied without the need for a reference to be made. This would assist in the workload of the ECJ and perhaps is overdue in that the national courts affected by the principle are those which contain experienced and well qualified judges. However, the ECJ did give a warning to those who wished to apply the principle of *acte clair*. They should remember that although the matter may be obvious to them, is it equally obvious to the courts in other Member States and the ECJ itself? The Court specifically mentioned three particular difficulties:

1. Community legislation is drafted in several languages and that the different language versions are all equally authentic. Any interpretation therefore involves the comparison of different language versions.
2. Community law uses terminology which is peculiar to itself and some legal concepts do not necessarily have the same meaning in Community law or in the various Member States.
3. Every provision of Community law must be placed in its context and interpreted in the light of provisions of Community law as a whole. (See Interpretation above, p.26).

Having made these points the Court came to the conclusion in *CILFIT* that Art.234(3) EC (ex 177(3) EC) does place an obligation to refer on the court *unless* it was established that the question raised is irrelevant or has already been interpreted or that the correct application of Community law is so obvious as to leave no scope for any reasonable doubt. However, the national court still remains entirely at liberty to make a reference if it wishes. In the UK the House of Lords has adopted the approach recommended by the ECJ in *CILFIT*.

Guidelines and Procedures used in the English Courts

As was stated above the national courts cannot be fettered by national rules when it comes to exercising their rights to make a preliminary reference. Having accepted this principle a number of guidelines have been given to help the court or tribunal decide whether or when to make a reference. Lord Denning in

Bulmer v Bollinger was the first senior judge to provide some guidance for lower courts. He said that the following facts should be taken into account:

(a) the facts should be decided first, so that the question of whether it was "necessary" could be settled;
(b) the reference to Luxembourg will cause delay and therefore add to the costs of the parties, so the lower court should deal with the case and leave it to an appeal court to decide whether or not to make a reference;
(c) the difficulty or importance of the question;
(d) the wishes of the parties should be taken into account, although it was the courts decision whether to make a reference or not;
(e) the need to avoid overloading the ECJ.

These guidelines are still used by the English Courts, although they have been clarified by other judges. See MacPherson J. in *R. v HM Treasury, Ex p. Daily Mail & General Trust Plc* [1989] 1 All E.R. 328, Kerr L.J. in *R. v The Pharmaceutical Society of GB, Ex p. the Association of Pharmaceutical Importers* [1987] 3 C.M.L.R. 951 and Bingham M.R. in The Stock Exchange case (1993).

Rules of the Supreme Court Order 114

Once a court of tribunal has decided to make a reference the procedure for it to made in England is provided by the RSC Order 114. The court frames the questions it wishes answered and the Senior Master sends a copy to the Registrar of the European Court. There is sometimes a delay where the reference is being made by the High Court, to allow for any appeal against the reference to be made to the Court of Appeal. While a reply is awaited from the ECJ the proceedings in the national court are stayed.

Effects of a Preliminary Ruling

The national court or tribunal which made the reference may actually decide the case on other grounds, but if it does apply Community law it is bound by the ruling of the ECJ. As far as other courts are concerned they may accept the interpretation in the ruling makes it unnecessary for them to make their own reference on the same point of Community law, but they can still make a separate reference if they wish.

Refusal of a Preliminary Reference

The ECJ recognises that the preliminary reference procedure has an important contribution to make towards the co-operation it seeks to develop with national courts. It is very rare for the ECJ to refuse a reference if the court or tribunal making it comes within Art.234 EC (ex 177 EC). However, in the *Foglia v Novello* cases (Cases 104/79 and 244/80 respectively) the Court refused a reference because it felt that there was an absence of any real legal dispute between the parties. It was felt that this case would herald a restrictive approach by the ECJ but this has not happened. In Case 150/88 *Parfumerie-Fabrik v Provide* the ECJ confirmed that it would not lightly infer an absence of a genuine dispute between the parties. In Case 83/91 *Meilicke v ADV/ ORGA FA Meyer* the Court ruled that "the spirit of cooperation which must prevail in preliminary ruling proceedings requires the national court to have regard to the function entrusted to the Court of Justice, which is to contribute to the administration of justice in member states and not give opinions on general or hypothetical questions".

Preliminary Rulings on Validity

In Case 314/85 *Foto-Frost v Hauptzollamt Lubeck Ost* the ECJ held that national courts were entitled to find that acts adopted by the institutions of the Community were valid, but they had no power in normal proceedings to declare such acts invalid. This is to stop them placing in jeopardy the unity of the Community legal order and would detract from the fundamental requirement of legal certainty. The only exception to this would possibly be in interlocutory proceedings.

5. JUDICIAL REMEDIES AND REVIEW

ENFORCEMENT ACTIONS BY THE EUROPEAN COMMISSION

In Case 6/64 *Costa v ENEL* the Court of Justice stressed the point that the Community was a new legal order which required Community law to obeyed. If this did not happen the "legal basis of the Community itself would be called into question". There needs to be, therefore, a mechanism for forcing the Member States to fulfil their obligations under the Treaty. As was stated in Chapter 2 above, p.9, the European Commission have been given the general duty under Art.211 EC (ex 155 EC) to "ensure that the provisions of this Treaty and the measures taken by the institutions pursuant thereto are applied". The Commission has been given this power under Art.226 EC (ex 169 EC).

The Art.226 EC (ex 169 EC) procedure can be initiated whenever the Commission considers that a Member State has failed to fulfil an obligation under the Treaty. This would include breach of administrative acts, general principles of Community law or international agreements. The breach may take the form of either an act or an omission such as the non-implementation of EC law or the retention of national laws which conflict with EC law. One of the problems for the Commission is that they receive many complaints that Member States are failing to fulfil their obligations. They come from individuals, companies, trade unions, pressure groups, MEPs and even from other governments. Member States have a legal duty to co-operate with the Commission investigations into alleged breaches by them (Case 45/93 *Commission v Spain*).

There are two stages to the procedure; an administrative stage and a judicial stage. The administrative stage is where the Director-General responsible for the policy of the Community will write to the Member State informing it that the Commission has formed the view that their is a breach of an obligation under the Treaty. Obviously there has been some investigation by the Director-General's office before this happens. The Member State then has an opportunity to answer the allegations or rectify the position. This is a very delicate stage because no government likes to be considered in breach of a treaty obligation. If after receiving a reply from the Member State the Commission considers that the Member State has been in breach it may deliver a reasoned opinion.

Reasoned Opinion

The reasoned opinion is a very important document because it will form the basis of the legal proceedings under Art.226 EC (ex 169 EC) if the Commission decides to go on to that stage. At this stage the reasoned opinion is considered confidential and is not legally binding and cannot be challenged (Case 4/69 *Alfons Lutticke GmbH v E.C. Commission No.1*). It has two purposes:

1. It must set out the reasons of facts and law for which the Commission considers that the Member State concerned has failed to fulfil its obligations; and
2. It must inform the State of the measures which the Commission considers necessary to bring the failure to an end.

The Treaty does not specify the time-scale in which this must take place, but a reasonable time must be given by the Commission. The delivery of the reasoned opinion marks the end of the administrative stage.

The Commission has a discretion as to whether to take the procedure on to the next stage. Advocate-General Roemer in Case 26/69 *Commission v France* suggested a number of situations in which the Commission might be justified in not initiating the enforcement procedure. These included the possibility that an amicable settlement could be achieved if formal proceedings were delayed, or where the effects of the violation were only minor, or where there is a possibility that the Community provision in question might be altered in the near future. Other situations which have been put forward is where the breach is the isolated act of an official or where action might inflame a politically sensitive situation. It is interesting to note that no action has been brought against the violation of Community law by national courts, even in situations like the *Cohn-Bendit* judgment in 1978. This is perhaps due to the fear that such an action might be seen as undermining the independence of the judiciary (See *Syndicat General de Fabricants de Semoules de France* [1970] C.M.L.R 395).

Interim Measures

An application for interim relief can be made to the ECJ at any time once the administrative stage of the Art.226 EC (ex 169 EC) procedure has been completed. Art.243 EC (ex 186 EC) states that "The Court of Justice may in any cases brought before it prescribe any necessary interim measures". In such situations the European Commission must show that a *prima facie* case is made out and that the urgency of the situation requires action by the Court.

Judicial Stage

If the Member State has not rectified its breach and the time period has elapsed, the Commission may bring the matter before the ECJ. This would indicate that the Commission has a discretion at this stage. However, the duty under Art.211 EC (ex 155 EC) mentioned above must be remembered. The duty requires the Commission to take appropriate action to ensure that the breach is rectified. Every attempt will be made to reach an amicable settlement.

The Court will consider whether the violation specified in the reasoned opinion has taken place. The Commission cannot raise new violations at the judicial stage. However, the Commission can continue with the action even if the Member State has terminated its infringement during the judicial stage, as happened in Case 7/61 *Commission v Italy* (*Pork Imports* case). The Member States put forward many reasons for their failure, some of them quite ingenious. These have included the inability of the national government to get the required legislation through their national parliaments or where trade union pressure prevented the Member State (*Commission v UK*).

ENFORCEMENT ACTIONS BY A MEMBER STATE

Generally the governments of Member States are prepared to leave breaches of Community obligations by other Member States to the Commission to seek enforcement under Art.226 EC (ex 169 EC). It is only in exceptional situations that a Member State will take on the responsibility itself, but if it does it has the procedure under Art.227 EC (ex 170 EC) to follow. The applicant Member State has to report the breach to the Commission, which will give the defaulting Member State an opportunity to make representations and carry out its own investigations. If the Commission has not issued a reasoned opinion within three months, the Member State complaining of the breach may bring the matter before the ECJ. It may be that a Member State wants to make a particular political point and for that reason brings the action under Art.227 EC (ex 170 EC) rather than leaving it to the Commission's procedure (Case 141/78 *France v UK*).

Remedy under Art.228 EC (ex 171 EC)

Whether the action against a Member State is brought under Arts 226 or 227 EC (ex 169 or 170 EC), the remedy provided is that of Art.228 EC (ex 171 EC). Originally the remedy was only a declaration by the Court that the Member State was in default and that it should take the necessary steps to comply with the judgment of the Court. On some occasions this meant that if the Member State continued with the breach the whole procedure had to be started again. However, this was changed by the Maastricht Treaty on European Union with regards to actions under Art.226 EC (ex 169 EC). Now if the Commission considers that the Member State has continued with the breach, it may issue a reasoned opinion after allowing the Member State to make their observations. The reasoned opinion must specify the points where the Member State has not complied with the Court's judgment and give a time limit for compliance to be achieved. If this does not happen the Commission may being the matter before the Court again, but this time specifying an appropriate lump sum or penalty to be paid by the Member State. If the Court considers that the Member State has not complied with its judgment, it may impose a lump sum or penalty. In January 1997 the Commission agreed a procedure so that it could recommend to the Court the appropriate fine based on a daily fine multiplied by the gravity and the time duration of the breach. In Case 387/97 *Commission v Hellenic Republic* the Court ordered Greece to pay a daily fine of 20,000 euros for its failure to meet its obligations under Directive 75/442 on toxic waste.

There are a number of "mays" in the amended Art.226 EC (ex 171 EC) and there was some doubt as to what would happen when the Commission or the Court decided to exercise the new powers given to them. In 1996 the first fines were imposed and the ECJ has noted "that the use of fines has led to a more uniform, complete and simultaneous application of Community law rules in all Member States". However, there continues to be a discretion exercised by the Commission, illustrated by its decision in November 2002 not to take France back to the Court to be fined for the breach associated with the BSE issue surrounding the export of beef from the UK to France.

Action for Annulment under Art.230 EC (ex 173 EC)

The action under Art.230 EC (ex 173 EC) is a direct challenge upon the validity of a Community act. There are five grounds on which the challenge can be based, the sole purpose of which is to get the act annulled. In any annulment proceedings the ECJ has no other option but to annul or not to annul. It cannot replace the act or amend it. The exception to this is where the Court can declare a regulation void but decide that the particular effects accomplished by it shall remain valid even if only temporary. This provides time for the Commission or Council to rectify the situation.

Which Acts can be Challenged?

The amended Art.230 EC (ex 173 EC) gives the Court the authority to review the legality of all those acts specified in Art.249 EC (ex 189 EC) which are intended to be legally binding. Therefore opinions and recommendations are not covered as they are not legally binding. The acts covered include those of the Council, the Commission, the European Parliament and the European Central Bank. However, there is some flexibility.

The most important requirement in any action under this article is that the measure being challenged should be legally binding. Thus in Case 22/70 *EC Commission v EC Council* (the *ERTA* case) the Commission had started actions under Art.230 EC (ex 173 EC) for the annulment of the Council's discussions resulting in a common position. The Commission disagreed with the procedure adopted by the Council for the negotiations for the European Road Transport Agreement because they felt that this was now a matter for the Community and not the individual Member States. The main point of the case concerned who had competence with regard to external agreements on this policy area. The ECJ held that "it would be inconsistent with the objectives [of the Article] to interpret the conditions under which an action is admissible so restrictively as to limit the availability of this procedure merely to the categories of measures referred to by Art.249 EC (ex 189 EC)". The Court's judgment in ERTA was followed in the more recent Case 294/83 *Les Verts v Parliament* where a French political grouping sought the annulment of two measures adopted by the European Parliament.

Privileged Applicants

Under Art.230(2) EC (ex 173(2) EC) the Member States, the Council or the Commission can challenge any legally binding act. They do not have to show any specific *locus standi*. The European Parliament made a number of attempts to be accepted by the Court as being within this same category of privileged applicants on the basis that its status had become more important since direct elections. In Case 70/88 *European Parliament v Council* (the *Chernobyl* case) the ECJ held that Parliament had the right to seek annulment of acts adopted by the Council and the Commission where the purpose of the proceedings was to protect the Parliament's prerogatives. Under the provisions of the Treaty on European Union, the Article has been amended to allow for actions by both the EP and the ECB for "the purpose of protecting their prerogatives". The case brought by Les Verts against the Parliament mentioned above would now come under Art.230(3) EC (ex 173(3) EC).

Non-privileged Applicants

This category of applicant includes all those listed in Art.230(4) EC (ex 173(4) EC), namely any natural or legal person. The ability of these individuals to challenge Community acts are severely restricted, in contrast to the "privileged applicants". They may only bring proceedings against three types of act, namely;

(a) a decision addressed to the applicant;
(b) a decision in the form of a regulation which is of direct and individual concern to the applicant;
(c) a decision addressed to another person which is of direct and individual concern to the applicant.

This shows that if a decision is addressed to an individual, as would happen, *e.g.* in competition policy cases, he may challenge it before the Court under this procedure. There is no mention of directives in the list, but it has been argued before the ECJ that directives are decisions addressed to the Member States. Therefore they could come within (c) above. The main points which need to be resolved is to clarify what amounts to a "decision in the form of a regulation" and "direct and individual concern".

A Decision in the Form of a Regulation

The title of the particular Community act is not decisive, therefore because it is called a "regulation" it will not automatically bar the action. It is the content and not the form which is important. A regulation under Art.249 EC (ex 189 EC) is essentially of a legislative nature and is applicable to a number of persons viewed abstractly and in their entirety. In the *Fruit & Vegetables* case the Court held that "a measure which is applicable to objectively determined situations and which involves immediate legal consequences in all Member States for categories of persons viewed in a general and abstract manner cannot be considered as constituting a decision".

A regulation does not lose its character as a regulation simply because it may be possible to ascertain the number or even the identity of the persons to which it applies at any given time. (See Case 6/68 *Zuckerfabrik Watenstedt v Council* and Case 789/79 *Calpak SpA v Commission*). In Case 25/62 *Plaumann & Co v EEC Commission* case the ECJ stated that "it follows from Articles 249 EC and 254 EC (ex 189 and 191 EC) that decisions are characterised by the limited number of persons to whom they are addressed".

If the ECJ concludes that the act is a true regulation then it can not be challenged under Art.173 EC, but the individual may seek a remedy within their national courts.

Direct and Individual Concern

The inclusion of this phrase in the Article has severely restricted the possibilities for it to be used by an individual who is seeking to challenge a decision not addressed to them.

Direct Concern This is interpreted by the Court to mean that the addressee is left no latitude of discretion so that the decision affects the applicant without the addressee being required to take any decision himself. In the *Toepfer* case mentioned below the applicant was directly concerned because the decision was addressed to the German government, who could not alter its application. When the Japanese companies challenged the Community rules on ball bearings the action was admissible because the national implementing measures were purely automatic (see *Japanese Ball-Bearing* cases, *e.g.* Cases 113/77 and 119–121/77).

In the *Chinese Mushrooms* case (Case 62/70 *Werner A. Bock v EC Commission*) the fact that the German authorities had already made up their mind to reject the applicant's request when they had authorisation to do so from the Commission, made the matter of direct concern to the applicant.

The notion of direct concern has some similarities with that of direct effect. In both cases the government of the Member State has no discretion and the act is of legal relevance to individuals who need not be the addressee of the decision.

Individual Concern   Plaumann, an importer of clementines, instituted proceedings against a decision addressed to the German government by the Commission, refusing them permission to suspend the collection of import duties on the fruit. Plaumann claimed that as he was required to pay the duty he was "individually concerned". The ECJ disagreed when it held,

> "Persons other than those to whom a decision is addressed may only claim to be individually concerned if that decision affects them by reason of certain attributes which are peculiar to them or by reason of circumstances in which they are differentiated from all other persons and by virtue of these factors distinguishes them individually just as in the case of the person addressed".

As any importer would be affected in the same way as Plaumann, he was not distinguished sufficiently to put him in the same category as the German government who received the decision.

However, in the first *Toepfer* case a decision addressed to the German government was considered to be of individual concern to the applicant. In this case the number of importers involved was in the past and therefore fixed as no new names could be added to the list. The Court said that "this created differentiates the said importers . . . from all other persons and distinguishes them individually just as in the case of the person addressed". (See also Case 100/74 *CAM SA v EC Commission* (the *CAM* case)).

It would appear from the case law of the Court that a natural or legal person can only claim to be individually concerned when he disputes an act concerning a period in the past and which affects an identifiable group of persons, to which the applicant belongs.

Despite statements in *Plaumann* that Art.230 EC (ex 173 EC) should not be interpreted too restrictively, the number of successful actions by private individuals where the decision is not addressed to them is very small. Perhaps the ECJ may be in the process of changing this view (See Case 358/89 *Extramet Industrie v Council*). In Case 50/00 *Union de Pequenos Agricultores v EC Council* Advocate-General Jacobs suggested that where an individual would have no other possible remedy, it was only just that their action should be heard under Art.230 EC. This was followed by the Court of First Instance in Case 177/01 *Jego-*

Quere et Cie SA v Commission also supporting reform. However, the Court of Justice reiterated in the judgment in *Union de Pequenos Agricultores* that the *Plaumann* test should apply and it was the national courts to provide a remedy if the individual did not satisfy the test for an action under Art.230 EC. However, if the individual can satisfy the test for *locus standi* they still have to prove one of the five grounds specified in the second paragraph of the Article if the measure is to be annulled.

Grounds for Annulment

The grounds for illegality must have been present at the time the decision was taken. There are five such grounds, although they have gradually lost their individual importance. The case law of the Court would seem to indicate that the ECJ is not concerned with the specific ground of illegality. The most common grounds pleaded are "infringement of this Treaty or of any rule of law relating to its application".

1. *Lack of Competence*—The institutions of the Community have no general powers and may only act where the Treaty expressly attributes competence to them. This idea is similar to that of *ultra vires* in English law.
2. *Infringement of an essential Procedural requirement*—For the purposes of annulment of an act three procedural requirements have been identified as essential. These are (a) that the required advice must have been sought, *e.g* from the European Parliament; (b) the acts must be reasoned, and (c) the acts must have been published. (See Case 139/79 *Maizena GmbH v EC Council* and Case 138/79 *SA Roquette Frere v EC Council* where the opinion of the European Parliament was not received before the Council acted. The result was that the measure was annulled.)
3. *Infringement of this Treaty*—This is the most important ground as virtually any error by a Community institution can be viewed as a violation of the Treaty. Therefore this ground is the most widely used and is one which has been the most often successful.
4. *Infringement of any rule of law relating to the application of this Treaty*—The ECJ has stated that this includes all rules of Community law other than those found in the Treaty. It therefore includes all the general principles of Community law.

5. *Misuse of Powers*—Derived from French administrative law this ground covers those situations where a power is used for a purpose other than that for which it was granted, *i.e.* an improper purpose. Unlike the other grounds of invalidity, which are objective in character, the misuse of powers is subjective. It is therefore difficult to prove.

Time Limits

Under Art.230(5) EC (ex 173(5)) proceedings must be instituted "within two months of the publication of the measure, or of its notification to the plaintiff, or, in the absence thereof, of the day on which it came to the knowledge of the latter, as the case may be."

Effect of the Annulment

The remedy for actions under Art.230 EC (ex 173 EC) is stated in Art.231 EC (ex 174 EC):

"If the action is well founded, the Court of Justice shall declare the act concerned to be void. In the case of a regulation, however, the Court of Justice shall, if it considers this necessary, state which of the effects of the regulation which it has declared void shall be considered as definitive".

Thus the measure will be declared *erga omnes*, as if it never existed. Under Art.233 EC (ex 176 EC) the institution whose act has been declared void must take the necessary measures to comply with the judgment of the Court. If the successful applicant has suffered financial loss he may seek damages under Art.288(2) EC (ex 215(2) EC).

Action for Failure to Act

This action, which is often called the appeal against inaction, is founded upon Art.232 EC (ex 175 EC). Although it is rarely used, its potential use is against the Council or Commission and the European Parliament. As with Art.230 EC (ex 173 EC) mentioned above there are the two classes of applicant, the privileged and the non-privileged. The Article requires that the defaulting institution must first be called upon to act. If after two months the institution concerned has not defined its position, the action may be brought after a further two months. The remedy for the action is contained in Art.233 EC (ex 176 EC), *i.e.* the institution should act.

The ECJ has concluded that the obvious similarities between Arts 230 and 232 EC (ex 173 and 175 EC) mean that the two Articles are concerned essentially with the same remedy. This is referred to as the "unity principle". Therefore an individual cannot use one against the other. For example in the first *Lutticke* case the applicant invoked Art.232 EC (ex 175 EC) and called upon the Commission to initiate proceedings against the German government under Art.226 EC (ex 169 EC). When they replied that there was no violation of Art.90 EC (ex 95 EC) by Germany, Lutticke brought an action under Art.230 EC (ex 173 EC) to have the reply annulled. The Court said that neither action was admissible as the Commission's reply was not a reviewable act and that by sending it they had acted so Art.232 EC (ex 175 EC) did not apply. Also in Case 289/97 *Eridania SpA v Azienda Agricola San Luca di Rumagnoli Viannj*, the applicant failed under Art.230 EC (ex 173 EC) because he was not directly and individually concerned. He asked for the acts to be repealed and when after two months they had not been he brought an action under Art.232 EC (ex 175 EC). The Court refused to consider Art.232 EC (ex 175 EC) because it would have allowed the applicant to have circumvented the conditions of Art.230 EC (ex 173 EC).

Plea of Illegality

The plea of illegality under Art.241 EC (ex 184 EC) is designed to prevent the application of an illegal act from being used as a legal basis for further action. It specifically refers to the fact that it applies when the time period mentioned in Art.230(5) EC (ex 173(5) EC) would otherwise bar an action. The Article refers to "any party" being able to plead illegality, which would include both privileged and non-privileged applicants discussed above. Thus Art.241 EC (ex 184 EC) does not give a right of action in itself, but can be pleaded in other actions, such as annulment or failure to act or those for damages under Art.288(2) EC (ex 215(2) EC).

The Article refers specifically to regulations but as with Art.230 EC (ex 173 EC) above the Court is concerned with the substance rather than the form. Art.241 EC (ex 184 EC) is very rarely used because it can only be pleaded in actions before the ECJ, which have very narrow *locus standi* for non-privileged applicants. It is not necessary to use the plea in domestic proceedings as under Art.234(1)(b) EC (ex 177(1)(b) EC) the validity of a Community act, including regulations, can be raised.

Remedies Available Before the National Courts

A request for a preliminary ruling on the validity of a Community act can be brought by national courts when they have to apply a Community act whose validity is doubted. This is done under the procedure of Art.234(1)(b) EC (ex 177(1)(b) EC). It obviates the situation where national courts would otherwise be obliged to apply invalid rules of Community law. However, the ECJ refused in Case 188/92 *TWD Textilwerke Deggendorf GmbH v Germany* to declare on the validity of a Commission decision because the applicants had been informed by the German government of their rights of challenge under Art.230 EC.

As was held by the Court in Case 479/93 *Andrea Francovich v Italian Republic* it is also possible to obtain damages in the national courts. (See Chapter 3 above, p.37).

Damages under Art.288 EC (ex 215 EC)

Art.235 EC (ex 178 EC) gives the ECJ exclusive jurisdiction to hear cases relating to compensation for tortious damage under Art.288(2) EC (ex 215(2) EC). Contractual liability of the Community is governed by the law applicable to the contract in question.

The Court is instructed to decide cases of tortious liability in accordance with the general principles common to the laws of the Member States. In this way it is intended to make good any damage caused by Community institutions or by its servants in the performance of their duties. Unfortunately the Court has adopted a very restrictive approach towards the tortious liability of the Community, although there have been some successes (see Case 145/83 *Adams v Commission*).

Liability under Art.288(2) EC (ex 215(2) EC) can extend to liability in respect of legislation. The Case 5/71 *Zuckerfabrik Schoppenstedt v Council* developed certain guidelines for such situations. The court said that the non-contractual liability of the Community presupposes at the very least the unlawful nature of the act alleged to be the cause of the damage. No non-contractual liability will arise involving measures of economic policy unless a sufficiently flagrant violation of a superior rule of law for the protection of the individual has occurred. Having set this principle the court had to decide whether such a violation had actually occurred in this case.

Analysing this sentence "a superior rule of law for the protection of individuals" includes any general principle of Community law. This would include such examples as equality or proportionality. The requirement that there should be a "sufficiently flagrant" or serious violation has been narrowly construed by the court. In the joined Cases 83 and 94/76 and 4, 15 and 40/77 of *Bayerische HNL Vermehrungsbetriebe GmbH v Council and Commission* the court stated that no liability would be incurred by the Community institutions unless the institution concerned had manifestly and gravely disregarded the limits on the exercise of its power. In subsequent cases the court's view has been that the breach must be both serious and inexcusable.

Limitation Period

Actions under Art.288(2) EC (ex 215(2) EC) are subject to a limitation period of five years.

---

6. FREE MOVEMENT OF GOODS

An essential element of the common market is the series of freedoms which constitute the "foundations of the Community". Of these freedoms the most important is the free movement of goods which also includes agricultural product.

The Treaty does not provide a definition of the concept "common market", but Art.23 EC (ex 9(1) EC) states that:

> "The Community shall be based upon a customs union which shall cover all trade in goods and which shall involve the prohibition between Members States of customs duties on imports and exports and of all charges having equivalent effect, and the adoption of a common customs tariff in their relations with third countries."

The latter differentiates between a customs union and a free trade area, such as EFTA or NAFTA, which has no common customs tariff and is therefore limited to free movement of products originating in states belonging to the trade area.

The customs union was completed on June 30, 1968 for the original Member States. It was given effect by two essential measures:

1. Abolition of customs duties between Member States, and
2. Full application of the common customs tariff.

In order to create a single internal market of the whole Community it was necessary to remove the economic frontiers and legal obstacles to transnational trade. In theory the operation was based on the twin principles of free circulation of goods and non-discrimination between domestic and foreign products of the Member States. In that sense exports and imports as between Member States have become only a matter of domestic accounting as far as individual Member States are concerned. In fact the information on trade is now collected by the Commission. In practice the ECJ initially insisted on the enforcement of both principles, but seems now to be content to enforce the principle of free circulation which was given a broad meaning.

Thus the Treaty envisages the Community based on a Customs Union. This concept rests upon Arts 23 and 90 EC (ex 9 and 95 EC).

Art.23 EC (ex 9 EC)—enumerates the elements necessary to achieve a customs union.

Art.90 EC (ex 95 EC)—prohibits internal taxation on imports having an equivalent effect to customs duties.

Free Circulation

Goods benefiting from the right to free circulation are the products originating from Member States as well as products coming from non-Member States which are in free circulation in that Member State. "Products coming from a third country shall be considered to be in free circulation in a Member State if the import formalities have been complied with and any customs duties or charges having equivalent effect which are payable have been levied in that Member State," Art.24 EC (ex 10(1) EC).

Elimination of Duties between Member States

This was a formidable task because it was not merely a question of clearing up the jungle of national customs laws but basically of overcoming the idea of Member States being sovereign economic units. To ensure an immediate effect Art.25 EC (ex 12 EC) prohibits the increase of existing customs duties and the imposition of new duties on imports and exports or any charges having an equivalent effect. (See *Van Gend en Loos*).

Charges Having Equivalent Effect

Whilst the illegality of customs duties, export taxes and levies is a straightforward proposition "charges having an equivalent effect" prohibited by Art.25 EC (ex 12 EC) have posed a continuous problem as they are often subtle in execution. Although they are not defined by the Treaty, the ECJ defined these charges as "duties whatever their description or techniques imposed unilaterally, which apply specifically to a product imported by a Member State, but not to a similar national product and which by altering the price, have the same effect upon the free movement of goods as a customs duty". (Case 24/68 *Commission v Italy*.)

Examples

  (a) A statistical levy on imported goods—Case 7/68 *EC Commission v Italy*
  (b) A tax on cardboard egg containers charged to egg importer for the benefit of a national organisation set up for the promotion of production of paper and cellulose in Italy. (Case 94/74 *Industria Gomma v Ente Nazionale per la Cellulose*)

Both (a) and (b) are prohibited by the Treaty.

  (c) Charging 0.50 per cent *ad valorem* duty for administrative services in respect of goods imported from other MS. Italy was found to be guilty of a failure to fulfil an obligation under the Treaty.
  (d) More plausible charges such as for phyto-sanitary inspection of fruit or veterinary and public health inspection of meat are also prohibited unless authorised by the Community and applied accordingly.

It is not the test that is disapproved of, but the charge for the test. It would appear from the case law of the Court that a charge levied for a service rendered to the importer and which is not too general and uncertain would be permissible. This principle has, however, been given the narrowest possible scope. The ECJ has held that where an inspection service is imposed in the general interest, *e.g.* for health or safety purposes, or quality control, this cannot be regarded as a service rendered to the importer or exporter to justify the imposition of a charge.

Art.90 EC (ex 95 EC)

Similar to customs duties and equivalent charges are internal taxes which if imposed upon goods coming from a fellow MS would discriminate against such goods. Such taxes are prohibited by Art.90 (ex 95 EC) if they are in excess of taxes imposed upon similar domestic products. For example, a German importer of powered milk was able to resist the demand for a payment in lieu of a turnover tax from which a similar national product was exempted. (See also *Commission v France* and *Commission v Greece*).

Elimination of Quantitative Restriction

Having abolished customs duties the Treaty purports to eliminate quotas by prohibiting quantitative restrictions on imports (Art.28 EC (ex 30 EC)) and exports (Art.29 EC (ex 34 EC)). Quantitative restrictions have been interpreted by the ECJ "as any measure which amounts to a total or partial restraint on imports, exports or goods in transit (see Case 2/73 *Riseria Luigi Geddo v Ente Nazionale Risi*).

There are still problems, with Member States acting independently to manipulate trade for domestic reasons. In law they can no longer resort to protectionist measures either to regulate the influx of foreign goods as a matter of national policy or to respond to pressures from industries incapable of coping with foreign competition. There were many examples initially but it is now rare for countries to resort to quotas, *e.g.* UK potatoes, French sheep meat. However, covert quota systems might operate by means of an import licence requirement. A licensing system might in itself amount to a quantitative restriction, or alternatively, a measure of equivalent effect to a quantitative restriction. Even if the granting of the licence was a pure formality the requirement of such a licence to import would amount to a breach of Art.28 EC (ex 30 EC).

To offer States guidance as to the meaning and scope of "measures having equivalent effect" to quantitative restrictions the Commission passed Directive 70/50. Although this Directive was concerned with the transitional period of the Community and therefore no longer binding, it does offer a non-binding guideline as to the measures to be considered as having equivalent effect.

There are "measures equivalent to quantitative restrictions" prohibited but not defined by the Treaty. To the surprise of Member States, both the Commission and the ECJ have been very generous in their interpretation of this term, to include not merely overtly protective measures or measures applicable only to imports (*i.e.* distinctly applicable measures), but measures applicable to imports and domestic goods alike (indistinctly applicable measures), often introduced for the best of motives. Such measures range from regulatory measures designed to enforce minimum standards, *e.g.* of size, weight, quality, price or content, to tests and inspections or certification requirements to ensure that goods conform to these standards, to any activity capable of influencing the behaviour of traders such as promoting goods by reason of their national origin (Case 113/80 *Commission v Ireland* (the *Buy Irish Campaign* Case).

Dassonville Formula

In 1974 the ECJ had the opportunity in *Dassonville* (the *Scotch whisky* case) to provide its own definition of measures having equivalent effect to quantitative restrictions. This definition, known as the *Dassonville* formula, has since been applied consistently. According to the formula:

> "All trading rules enacted by Member States which are capable of hindering, directly or indirectly, actually or potentially, intra-Community trade are to considered as measures having effect equivalent to quantitative restrictions."

Thus it is not necessary to show actual effect on trade between Member States as long as the measure is capable of such effects.

The measure in issue in *Dassonville* was a requirement, under Belgian law, that imported goods should carry a certificate of origin issued by the State in which the goods were manufactured. Dassonville imported a consignment of Scotch whisky from France. Since the sellers were unable to supply the required certificate he attached a home-made certificate of origin to the goods and appeared before the Belgian court on a forgery charge. In his defence, he claimed that the Belgian regulation was contrary to EC law. On a reference from the Belgian court under Art.234 EC (ex 177 EC), the ECJ, applying the above formula, found that the measure was capable of breaching Art.28 EC (ex 30 EC).

Cassis de Dijon Case

The ECJ took another decisive step in the case of *Cassis de Dijon* (Case 120/78 *Rewe-Zentral AG v Bundesmonopolverwaltung fur Branntwein*). This made a distinction between distinctly and indistinctly applicable measures. The question before the ECJ concerned the legality under EC law of a German law laying down a minimum alcohol level of 25 per cent for certain spirits, which included cassis, a blackcurrant-flavoured liqueur. German cassis complied with this minimum, but French cassis, with an alcohol content of 15–20 per cent did not. Thus although the German regulation was indistinctly applicable, the result of the measure was effectively to ban French cassis from the German market. A number of German importers contested the measure, and the German court referred a number of questions to the ECJ under Art.234 EC (ex 177 EC).

The ECJ applied the *Dassonville* formula above but added:

> "Obstacles to movement within the Community resulting from disparities between the national laws relating to the marketing of the products in question must be accepted in so far as those provisions may be recognised as being necessary in order to satisfy mandatory requirements relating in particular to the effectiveness of fiscal supervision, the protection of public health, the fairness of commercial transactions and the defence of the consumer."

This has subsequently been called the first Cassis principle, *i.e.* that certain measures will not breach Art.28 EC (ex 30 EC) if they are necessary to satisfy mandatory requirements even though they may come within the *Dassonville* formula because they are indistinctly applicable. If the measure is distinctly applicable it will normally breach Art.28 EC (ex 30 EC) but may be justified under Art.30 EC (ex 36 EC).

Thus in the *Cassis* case the ECJ found that the German law was in breach of Art.28 (ex 30 EC). Although the measure was allegedly enacted in the interests of public health (to prevent increased consumption resulting from lowering the alcoholic content of cassis) and the fairness of commercial transactions (to avoid giving the weak imported cassis an unfair advantage over its stronger, hence more expensive German rival), the measure was not necessary to achieve these ends. Other means, such as labelling, which would have been less of a hindrance to trade could have been used to achieve the same ends.

The ECJ established another important principle in the *Cassis* case ("the second Cassis principle"). "There was no valid reason why, provided that goods have been lawfully produced and marketed in one of the Member States, they should not be introduced into any other Member State." This gives rise to a presumption that goods which have been lawfully marketed in another Member State will comply with the "mandatory requirements" of the importing State. This can be rebutted by evidence that further measures are necessary to protect the interest concerned. However, the burden of proving that a measure is necessary is a heavy one and the presumption will be very hard to rebut.

Price controls, resulting in the fixing of profit margins, may be regarded as a measure having an equivalent effect to quantitative restrictions on imports if they place imported goods at a disadvantage in relation to identical national products/goods, *e.g.* a Dutch licensed victualler prosecuted for selling liquor at prices below the minimum fixed by the national law, successfully raised a defence that the prosecution was contrary to Art.28 EC (ex 30 EC).

In Case 267/91 *Criminal Proceedings against Keck*, a case concerned with resale at a loss, the Court was anxious to discourage excessive use of Art.28 EC (ex 30 EC) with regard to "certain selling arrangements" which are non-discriminatory. Such arrangements apply to all affected traders in the territory of the Member State and affect all traders in the same manner in law and in fact. In doing so they fall outside of the scope of Art.28 EC (ex 30 EC). *Keck* was applied by the Court in Case 391/92 *Commission v Greece*, a case involving the sale of processed milk for infants. Although the national legislation might restrict the volume of sales the legislation satisfied the conditions laid down in *Keck* and consequently did not breach Art.28 EC (ex 30 EC).

Derogation under Art.30 EC (ex 36 EC)

Art.30 EC (ex 36 EC) allows Member States to legitimately limit the freedom of movement of goods and thus derogate from principles comprised in Arts 28 and 29 EC (ex 30–34 EC). Although the grounds in Art.30 EC (ex 36 EC) appear extensive they have been narrowly construed by the Court. They must not constitute a means of arbitrary discrimination or a disguised restriction on trade between Member States.

The grounds for derogation are—"public morality, public policy and public security; the protection of health and life of humans, animals or plants; the protection of national treasures possessing artistic, historic or archaeological value; or the protection of industrial and commercial property".

"Public Morality, Policy and Security"

These terms express "peculiar national values" and it is difficult to envisage a uniform Community application of a diversity of values. The ECJ recognised its limitations in dealing with public policy and decreed that a certain margin of appreciation maybe left to national authorities. However, it does not follow that these matters are reserved to the exclusive jurisdiction of Member States, but permits national law to derogate from the principle of free movement of goods to the extent that such derogation is and continues to be justified under Art.30 EC (ex 36 EC).

Public Morality Examples—compare pornographic material freely available in another Member State in *R. v Henn, R. v Darby* [1980] 2 All E.R. 166 with *Conegate Ltd v Customs & Excise Commissioners* [1987] Q.B. 254 which involved the seizure of a number of inflatable rubber love dolls imported from Germany.

Public Policy This ground, potentially wide, has been strictly construed, and has never succeeded as a basis for derogation under Art.30 EC (ex 36 EC).

Public Security This ground was successfully invoked in Case 72/83 *Campus Oil Ltd v Minister for Industry and Energy* to justify an Irish order requiring importers of petroleum oils to buy up to 35 per cent of their requirements of petroleum products from the Irish National Petroleum Co at prices fixed by the minister. The Irish government argued that it was justified on public security grounds, to maintain a viable refinery which would meet essential needs in times of crisis. This was accepted by the ECJ.

Protection of Public Health

The cases reveal devices used by Member States to raise revenue or to discriminate against imported products. The health protection plea seems to have been argued rather tenuously and it was the commercial aspect which characterised those cases. However, it is possible to envisage a legitimate and compelling use in some cases such as those involving health precautions against rabies or humanitarian considerations in the transport of livestock.

There have been a number of attempts to derogate from the Treaty under this heading, *e.g. Commission v UK (Re UHT Milk), Commission v UK (Re Imports of Poultry Meat)* and Case 42/82 *Commission v France (Re Italian Table Wines).*

If a charge is levied for the inspection it maybe considered as a charge having equivalent effect. If it is not prohibited by the Treaty and not seen as a way of raising revenue but actually seen to assist the flow of goods it maybe acceptable.

Protection of Industrial and Commercial Property

This includes patents, copyright and trademarks. Faced with the problem of such rights being used in order to frustrate the Community competition policy or to impede the free movement of goods the ECJ distinguished between the existence of rights and their use. Only a legitimate use, *i.e.* one which is compatible with the rules on competition and the free movement of goods is justified.

In the opinion of the Court

> "in as much as it provides an exception to one of the fundamental principles of the Common Market, Art.30 EC (ex 36 EC) in fact admits exceptions to the free movement of goods only to the extent to which such exceptions are justified for the purpose of safeguarding rights which constitute the specific subject matter of that property"

Case 119/75 *Terrapin (Overseas) Ltd v Terranova Industrie.* (See also Competition Policy in the next chapter).

---

7. COMPETITION POLICY

ROLE OF COMPETITION IN THE EUROPEAN COMMUNITY

From its very beginning the European Community has always accorded great importance to competition. In Pt One of the EC

Treaty, where the Principles or activities of the Community are listed, Art.3(g) EC states "a system ensuring that competition in the internal market is not distorted". This is reinforced by Art.4 EC (ex 3(a) EC), introduced by the TEU, which states that the Community is to be "conducted in accordance with the principle of an open market economy with free competition".

This emphasis on competition has two advantages. For the European Commission competition is the best stimulant of economic activity as it guarantees the widest possible freedom of action to all. Secondly it prevents the introduction within the internal market of any new obstacles to trade by individuals, undertakings or Member States now that old barriers have been removed. A strong competition policy can be used to fulfil the objectives of the Community, such as economic integration.

The Treaty does not define the concept of "competition", but it does refer to certain measures which interfere with competition and which are therefore prohibited, subject to exemptions granted by the Commission.

There are two dimensions to competition policy within a Member State, that of the national laws of the Member State and imposed upon that a system of Community law. The Community rules are administered and enforced by the national authorities, subject to the special role of the Commission in the field of competition policy. Good communications between the Commission and the national authorities are important to ensure uniformity and to avoid the danger of concurrent national and Community action. If the Commission takes action under the Community's competition rules, it has priority over any subsequent action taken in the national courts.

Art.81 EC (ex 85 EC) and Restrictive Practices

Art.81 EC (ex 85 EC) complements Art.82 EC (ex 86 EC), as they both seek to secure fair competition by curbing restraints on trade. The procedure for the application of these two Articles is set out in Regulation 17/62. Article 81 EC (ex 85 EC) is concerned with the effect on trade of various restrictive practices involving two or more undertakings, whilst Art.82 EC (ex 86 EC) is primarily concerned with monopolist situations. Both are concerned with the abuse rather than the existence of economic power. The Community claims extra-territorial jurisdiction in that even if the undertaking is established outside the Community the competition policy will still apply if its actions will affect trade between the Member States.

Art.81 EC (ex 85 EC) 1. The following shall be prohibited as incompatible with the common market: all agreements between undertakings, decisions by associations of undertakings and concerted practices which may affect trade between Member States and which have as their object or effect the prevention restrictions or distortion of competition within the common market, and in particular those which:

(a) directly or indirectly fix purchase or selling prices or any other trading conditions;
(b) limit or control production, markets, technical development, or investment;
(c) share markets or sources of supply;
(d) apply dissimilar conditions to equivalent transactions with other trading parties, thereby placing them at a competitive disadvantage;
(e) make the conclusion of contracts subject to acceptance by the other parties of supplementary obligations which, by their nature or according to commercial usage, have no connection with the subject of such contracts.

2. Any agreements or decisions prohibited pursuant to this Article shall be automatically void.
3. The provisions of paragraph 1 may, however, be declared inapplicable in the case of:

— any agreement or category of agreements between undertakings;
— any decision or category of decisions by associations of undertakings;
— any concerted practice or category of concerted practices;

which contributes to improving the production or distribution of goods or to promoting technical or economic progress, while allowing consumers a fair share of the resulting benefit, and which does not;

(a) impose on the undertakings concerned restrictions which are not indispensable to the attainment of these objects;
(b) afford such undertakings the possibility of eliminating competition in respect of a substantial part of the products in question.

Agreements and Concerted Practices There are clearly three parts to Art.81 EC (ex 85 EC). Article 81(1) EC (ex 85(1) EC) is concerned with agreements between undertakings and decisions by associations of undertakings. However, it goes further by the use of the term "concerted practices". This refers to behaviour and includes any "gentleman's agreement" which have not been put into writing. The Court defined concerted practices in Case 48/69 *ICI v Commission* (the *Dyestuffs* case) as "a form of co-ordination between enterprises that has not yet reached the point where there is a contract in the true sense of the word but which, in practice consciously substitutes a practical co-operation for the risks of competition". It may be that the similarity of actions by undertakings is coincidental, in which case they are not prohibited. It is only where they are planned as a result of some collusion or concentration that they are prohibited. The Commission does have problems in proving such arrangements where the evidence maybe circumstantial. However, the onus maybe on the undertakings to prove that they had not entered into such an arrangement (*Dyestuffs*). Article 81 EC (ex 85 EC) is not concerned with agreements between undertakings belonging to the same concern, such as a parent company and its subsidiaries. A business must have economic independence in order to qualify as an undertaking within Art.81 EC (ex 85 EC). (See Joined Cases 159/91 and 160/91 *Poucet v AGF*).

Whatever behaviour or agreement is involved the prohibition under this Article will not apply unless it has as its object or effect the prevention, restrictions or distortion of competition within the common market. This can arise when any kind of action by an undertaking directly effects the market and is detrimental to production or sales to purchasers or consumers because it limits freedom of choice. The ECJ has refined the meaning of distortion of competition by adding the phrase "to an appreciable extent". In this way the Court has shown that it is not really concerned with small affects by applying the de minimus rule. It is necessary under the guidelines from the Court to take into account the nature and quantity of the product covered by the agreement, the position and importance of the parties on the market for the products concerned, the isolated nature of the disputed agreement, the severity of the clauses limiting trade between Member States and the opportunities for commercial competition in the same product. The term "within the Community" does not necessarily refer to competition in several Member States or even all. If there is an adverse effect on competition in one single Member State it maybe considered as taking place within the Community and prohibited by the Article. There is also listed (a) to (e) examples of such behaviour or agreements.

Exemption   Article 81(2) EC (ex 85(2) EC) states quite clearly that anything prohibited by Art.81(1) EC (ex 85(1) EC) is automatically void. However, Art.81(3) EC (ex 85(3) EC) provides for the possibility of exemption. Exemption in individual cases may only be granted once the Commission has been notified of the agreement concerned and the four conditions of Art.81(3) EC (ex 85(3) EC) fulfilled. The exemption may not enter into force on a date earlier than the date of notification. They are issued for a specified period and can have conditions or obligations attached to them. They can be renewed but also revoked, sometimes with retroactive effect. As a result of the time-scale needed for the Commission to deal with individual claims for exemption, a number of block exemptions have been issued in the form of regulations. These cover such commercial activities as exclusive purchasing agreements, exclusive agency agreements, patent licensing and research and development agreements. If the undertakings can ensure that the clauses of the agreement are within that specified by the block exemption they will not risk being fined and do not need to notify the Commission of the agreement. The Commission also publishes notices, which are not binding, specifying agreements which in its view do not fall within Art.81(1) EC (ex 85(1) EC).

Negative Clearance and Comfort Letters

If an undertaking wishes to obtain official confirmation that an agreement is outside those prohibited by Art.81(1) EC (ex 85(1) EC), it can apply for negative clearance. The Commission will only grant such clearance on the basis of information in its possession. It would require a great deal of work on the part of the Commission before it could grant a declaration of inapplicability of Art.81(1) EC (ex 85(1) EC). To ease this workload and to speed up its decision-making processes, the Commission began to issue "comfort letters". These provide a quick informal way of providing assurance for the parties concerned. A comfort letter is a communication from the Commission to the effect that, in its opinion, the agreement either does not infringe Art.81(1) EC (ex 85(1) EC) or that if it does infringe the Article it is of a type that qualifies for exemption. The letter generally concludes with the statement that the Commission considers the "file closed". Such letters have been held by the Court to be outside the framework of Regulation 17/62 as they are only administrative letters and as such are not legally binding on national courts. (See the *Perfumes* cases, Case 99/79 *SA Lancome v Etos BV*). Also the Commission can reopen the file at any time.

All agreements or practices covered by Art.81(1) EC (ex 85(1) EC) must be notified to the Commission as failure to do so, for any reason, may result in heavy fines being imposed by the Commission. (See below, p.75).

Art.82 EC (ex 86 EC) and the Abuse of a Dominant Position

Art.86 EEC   Any abuse by one or more undertakings of a dominant position within the common market or in a substantial part of it shall be prohibited as incompatible with the common market in so far as it may affect trade between Member States. Such abuse may, in particular, consist in:

(a) directly or indirectly imposing unfair purchase or selling prices or unfair trading conditions;
(b) limiting production, markets or technical development to the prejudice of consumers;
(c) applying dissimilar conditions to equivalent transactions with other trading parties, thereby placing them at a competitive disadvantage;
(d) making the conclusion of contracts subject to acceptance by the other parties of supplementary obligations which, by their nature or according to commercial usage, have no connection with the subject of such contracts.

There are three essential ingredients to this Article. There must be a dominant position, an abuse of that position and that abuse must affect trade between the Member States.

Dominant Position   What is meant by dominance? The Court stated in Case 27/76 *United Brands v Commission* that it is "a position of economic strength enjoyed by an undertaking which enables it to prevent effective competition being maintained on the relevant market by giving it the power to behave to an appreciable extent independently of its competitors, customers and ultimately of its consumers". The Commission added in Case 62/86 *AKZO Chemie BV v Commission* "The power to exclude effective competition is not . . . in all cases coterminous with independence from competitive factors but may also involve the ability to eliminate or seriously weaken existing competitors or to prevent potential competitors from entering the market". The existence of a dominant position is a question of fact determined by the relevant market factors. There has to be a relevant market for Art.82 EC (ex 86 EC) to operate, but this is not always easy to define. For example in *United Brands* the Commission made a detailed analysis and concluded that the relevant market was the banana market, of which United Brands had a substantial share. The company argued that it was the fresh fruit market which was relevant, of which they had a much smaller share. The ECJ held that the banana market was in fact a distinct market because the characteristics of the consumers meant that the product was not interchangeable. In Case 6/72 *Europemballage and Continental Can v Commission* the problem of product substitution and the inability on the part of the Commission to define the relevant market led to the annulment of the Commission's Decision. (See also Case 333/94 *Tetra-Pak International v Commission*).

With regard to the territory of the relevant market there is no fixed geographical definition. It could be a worldwide market or a narrowly localised market. The important point is that the abuse of the dominant position must take effect in the common market or a substantial part of it (Case 68/78 *Liptons Cash Registers v Hugin*).

If there is an abuse of a dominant position under Art.82 EC (ex 86 EC) there is no exemption.

Enforcement of Competition Policy

The European Commission has a central role in enforcing the Community's competition policy through Directorate-General 4 (DG4) the department responsible. To fulfil its tasks the Commission enjoys substantial powers, subject to strict procedural requirements under Regulation 17/62 and a general duty of confidentiality. A breach of these duties can result in the annulment of the Commission's Decision by the ECJ and possibly a successful action for damages (Case 145/83 *Adams v Commission*).

Investigative Powers

If the Commission is to undertake market analysis to enable it to make a Decision it needs powers of investigation.

(a) The Commission can request all information which is necessary to enable it to carry out its task from governments, competent authorities in the Member State such as the Office of Fair Trading in the UK, undertakings and associations of undertakings.
(b) The Commission may conduct general enquiries into whole sectors of the economy if economic trends suggest that competition in the common market is being restricted or distorted.
(c) The Commission may undertake all necessary on-the-spot investigations including entering premises, examining and copying business records and conducting oral examinations.

Before undertaking such investigations the officials of the Commission are required to produce written authorisation in the form of a Decision specifying the subject matter and purpose of the investigations (see Case 136/79 *National Panasonic v Commission* and Case 46/87 *Hoechst v Commission*). The undertakings are required to comply with the legitimate demands from the Commission. If they fail to do so or give false information they may be fined, as information cannot be withheld even if it is self-incriminating. In Case 155/79 *AM & S v Commission*, the ECJ stated that it was possible to claim privilege for correspondence between a client and an independent lawyer, but not where the lawyer is employed "in-house".

Fines and Penalties

The Commission has power under Regulation 17/62 to impose fines for breaches of Arts 81 and 82 EC (ex 85 and 86 EC). These can be up to 1 million euros or 10 per cent of the undertaking's global turnover, whichever is the greater. The largest fine imposed to date has been that imposed by the Commission against those in the Vitamins Cartel in 2001 where a fine of over 855 million euros was imposed. In 2002 The European Commission imposed fines totalling 478 million euros on four companies which operated a long-running cartel on the market for plasterboard, a product which is widely used in the building industry and by DIY practitioners.

None of the fine is paid to the party injured by the anti-competitive activity. Such victims must seek a remedy in their national courts. The size of the fine will depend on factors such as the nature and duration of the infringement, the economic importance of the undertakings and whether the parties have already infringed the Community's competition policy. To provide more transparency in the calculation of fines the European Commission adopted a number of guidelines in 1997.

Interim Measures

Although not specifically granted under Regulation 17/62, the ECJ has held that interim measures can be granted provided they were:

(1) indispensable,
(2) urgent, and
(3) necessary to avoid serious or irreparable damage to the party seeking the action or where there is a situation which is intolerable to the public interest (see Case 792/79 *Camera Care v Commission*).

Competition Law and Property Rights

The ECJ has recognised that there has to be some protection given to owners of intellectual property rights such as patents or trademarks. If this were absent the incentive to advance technological developments would be removed. This is why Art.30 EC (ex 36 EC) provides derogation from Art.28 EC (ex 30 EC), as discussed above. The Court has managed to balance these rights, confirmed in Art.295 EC (ex 222 EC), with the need not to impair competition. The specific subject matter of the right has been identified and protected but its exercise may be restricted or limited by the Treaty. (See Joined Cases 56/64 and 58/64 *Consten and Grundig v Commission* and Case 24/67 *Parke Davis v Centrafarm*). For example the owner of a patent is entitled to his "reward" of a higher price when the goods are first put on the market. He cannot control their price or distribution by refusing parallel imports as this may affect trade between Member States.

However, the ECJ decision in Case 355/96 *Silhouette International v Hartlauer Hendelsgesellschaft* seemed to take a more restrictive view when interpreting the Trade Mark Directive 89/104. Silhouette was allowed to exercise its trademark rights to prevent the importation of its sunglasses from outside the EEA, where they had been sold at a lower price. The ECJ had decided that Silhouette's trademark rights had not been exhausted when they had sold the sunglasses to a retailer in Bulgaria and therefore outside the EEA. In the later case of Case

173/98 *Sebago Inc and Ancienne Maison Dubois et Fils SA v GB-UNIC SA* the ECJ confirmed its interpretation of the Directive, but did raise the possibility for the importer to show that the owner of the trademark had consented to the exhaustion of their rights. In the English case of *Zino Davidoff SA v A&G Imports Ltd* [2002] Ch. 109, where the facts concerned the importation of luxury perfumes, the trademark owner was held to have consented. The essential function of a trade mark is to guarantee to consumers the real origin of goods or services, as the ECJ recently stated in the *Arsenal* case (Case 206/01 *Arsenal Football Club Plc v Reed*).

Anti-competitive Behaviour by Governments

Public undertakings and similar bodies are in principle subject to the same rules on competition as private undertakings (Art.86 EC (ex 90 EC)). However, they are exempted to the extent necessary to perform the particular tasks assigned to them. The Commission supervises such undertakings to ensure that the development of trade between the Member States is not affected.

With regard to state aids, Art.87 EC (ex 92 EC) prohibits any aid that distorts or threatens to distort competition by favouring certain undertakings or the production of certain goods. However, Art.87(2) EC (ex 92(2) EC) states that certain aid is always permissible, *e.g.* if it has a social character, and Art.87(3) EC (ex 92(3) EC) that other aids maybe permissible, *e.g.* for areas with high unemployment. There is a procedure laid down by Art.88 EC (ex 93 EC) by which the Commission can allow or prevent such aids.

EC Merger Policy

The Commission originally sought to deal with the impact of mergers on Community competition policy by using Arts 81 EC (ex 85 EC) (Case 730/79 *Philip Morris v Commission*) and 82 EC (ex 86 EC) (*Continental Can*). In September 1990 Council Regulation 4064/89, known as the Merger Regulation came into force. This regulation applies to mergers involving enterprises with an aggregate worldwide turnover of more than five billion euros and where the aggregate Community turnover of each of at least two of the enterprises concerned is more than 250 million euros. Even when these thresholds are not met the merger may still be covered by Art.1(3) of Regulation 1310/97 where other turnover thresholds are specified. Such mergers are subject to examination by the European Commission, unless they are primarily within one Member State. (See the *Aerospatiale-Alenia-de-Haviland* case (Case IV/M53)). Regulation 1310/97 amended Regulation 4064/89 to facilitate greater procedural harmony in the assessment of different types of mergers.

Under Art.2(3) of the Regulation there is a two-stage test of compatibility. The initial consideration is whether the concentration "creates or strengthens a dominant position within the common market or a substantial part of it". If this is satisfied, the Commission is required to assess whether the merger will significantly impede effective competition within the Community. The Commission will then either clear the merger, allowing it to take place, or stop it from taking place. This is not an easy task as is evidenced by the recent decisions by the CFI that annulled Commission decisions because the Court was not satisfied with the economic analysis of the anti-competition effects produced by the Commission. (*Tetra Laval BV* (T-5/02) and Case T-77/02 *Schneider Electric SA v Commission*).

Remedies in the National Courts

The courts of the Member States can apply Arts 85 and 86 as they are directly effective. If the court applies the rule of reason devised by the ECJ to decide if the agreement is contrary to Art.81(1) EC (ex 85(1) EC) and comes to the conclusion that it does, it can only declare it void under Art.81(2) EC (ex 85(2) EC). Only the Commission can grant exemption under Art.81(3) EC (ex 85(3) EC) and impose fines under Regulation 17/62. The national court should grant the same remedies as would be available in similar actions under national law, including interlocutory proceedings. However, in *Garden Cottage Foods Ltd v Milk Marketing Board* [1984] A.C. 130, the House of Lords left it unclear as to whether a breach of Art.81 EC (ex 85 EC) could give rise to a remedy in damages.

8. FREE MOVEMENT OF WORKERS

The EU seeks to promote comprehensive economic integration and these provisions apply to all workers of the Member States, regardless of occupation.

Since a common market requires the removal of all obstacles to the free movement of the factors of production, the free movement of workers in the Community may be seen as simply a prerequisite to the achievement of an economic objective. The Treaties do not purport to establish an absolute freedom of migration in a general sense, but confine themselves to this economic activity. Eventually the object is to create a "common market in manpower", which would serve the purpose of moving labour to areas which reveal shortage of manpower and to solve the problem of unemployment in overpopulated areas. Whether such a simplistic view can still be held in the light of future enlargement is an important question.

However this policy does not only have economic implications. There are also social consequences. The Preamble of Regulation 1612/68 states:

> "The freedom of movement constitutes a fundamental right of workers and their families; mobility of labour within the Community must be one of the means by which the worker is guaranteed the possibility of improving his living and working conditions and promoting his social advancement, while helping to satisfy the requirements of the economy of the Member States".

The freedom of movement of workers is mainly based on the principle of non-discrimination on the ground of nationality, while the freedom of non-wage earners to move within the Community is, generally speaking, expressed by the right of establishment and the right to provide service. For the non-economically active three Directives were adopted in 1990. Directive 90/364 gives rights to persons of independent means and Directive 90/365 covers retired persons who do not satisfy Directive 1251/70. In addition there is Directive 90/366 which provides rights to students undertaking a vocational course at a university in another Member State whereby they can reside in the host Member State for the duration of their course. This Directive was later annulled by the Court (Case 295/90 *European Parliament v Council*) on the grounds that the legal base claimed by the Council was wrong so that the Parliament was merely consulted and the co-operation procedure was not utilised.

However, the Directive remained in force until it was replaced by Directive 93/96. For all these directives there is one common factor, which is that the individual who is seeking to enforce a right under them is not economically dependant upon the benefits system of the host Member State.

Treaty Provisions

Article 39 EC (ex 48 EC) states that workers of one Member State are to be free to move to another Member State to accept offers of employment actually made, and to remain in a Member State for the purposes of carrying on employment.

Article 40 EC (ex 49 EC) authorises legislation by the Council to eliminate administrative procedures likely to impede the movement of workers and to set up machinery for matching offers of employment in one Member State with available candidates in another.

Article 42 EC (ex 51 EC) empowers the European Council to legislate in the field of social security affecting migrant workers.

Directives concerned determine the scope and detailed rules for exercise of rights conferred directly by the Treaty. No exit or entry visas are required from EC nationals, only an identity card or a passport.

Concept of "Worker"

Article 39 EC (ex 48 EC) refers to "freedom of movement for workers" and Art.1 of Regulation 1612/68 on Freedom of Movement for Workers within the Community refers to the right to "take up an activity as an employed person", but neither give definitions. The Court has said that the words must be given their ordinary meaning and not interpreted restrictively. However, the concept only covers pursuit of effective and genuine activities. Provided that he pursues this effective and genuine activity the motives of the individual are not to be taken into account. In Case 66/85 *Lawrie-Blum v Land Baden-Wurttemberg* the ECJ suggested that the essential characteristics of a worker are of someone who performs services for another during a certain period of time and under the direction of another in return for remuneration. In the *Levin* case (Case 53/81) the Court held that those who worked part-time were included provided the work was "real" work and not nominal or minimal. (see Case 139/85 *Kempf v Staatssecretaris van Justitie*).

Regulation 1408/71 defines a worker as anyone who is insured either compulsory or voluntarily within the framework of a social security system of a Member State organised for the benefit of salaried employees.

The definition of "worker" in the Community sense rarely causes difficulty because if an economically active claimant under Art.39 EC (ex 48 EC) is not a worker, he is probably self employed in which case Art.43 or 49 EC (ex 52 or 59 EC) would apply. The ECJ has held that Arts 39, 43 and 49 EC (ex 48, 52 and 59 EC) are based on the same principles as far as entry, residence and non-discrimination on the grounds of nationality are concerned and so categorisation under Art.39 EC (ex 48 EC), as apposed to Art.43 or 49 EC (ex 52 or 59 EC), will rarely be crucial.

Removal of Restrictions

The Council issued Directive 68/360 on the abolition of restrictions on movements and residence for workers of the Member State and their families. Both Art.39 EC (ex 48 EC) and the Directive have been held by the ECJ to be directly effective. Thus they give individuals rights which the courts in the Member States must protect and enforce.

Art.39(3) EC (ex 48(3) EC) envisages the free movement of workers for pursuit of accepting employment but makes no mention of a right to move freely in search of employment. Directive 68/360 makes no reference to this point either, but it has been generously interpreted by the Court. In Case 48/75 *Procureur du Roi v Royer* the Court held that Art.3 of the Directive included the right of workers to enter the territory of a Member State and reside there for the purposes intended by the Treaty, in particular to look for or pursue an activity as an employed person. In the *Levin* case this right was limited to three months on the proviso that the individual could support themselves without recourse to public assistance. Also in Case 292/89 *R. v Immigration Appeal Tribunal, Ex p. Antonissen* the Court held that immigrants seeking employment had the right to enter another Member State and stay there for a sufficient period of time to find out about the job market opportunities and to find a job. In the UK six months is allowed for a "worker" to find a job although generally at least three months are given by Member States.

Right of Residence

A worker's right to a residence permit is implied once he has secured a job but if he finds no job or if he loses it voluntarily he cannot expect to be entitled to a residence permit. Thus a British subject continuously unemployed was not entitled to a renewal of his residence permit in the Netherlands—*Williams v Dutch Secretary of State* (1977).

The right of residence means the right to stay indefinitely in the host country. A worker cannot be expelled except in cases justifiable under derogation from the freedom of movement. (See Limitations below, p.85). The residence permit is issued for a period of five years but it is renewable. The permit is merely proof of the right granted by the Treaty which exists independently of the document.

Regulation 1251/70

As a corollary to the freedom of movement protected by Regulation 1612/68 and Directive 68/360, Regulation 1251/70 gives the worker the right to remain in the territory of a Member State after having been employed there. This right applies to the retired and the incapacitated worker. A worker acquires a right of residence on retirement provided that he has reached the age laid down in that Member State for entitlement to an old-age pension, has resided continuously in that Member State for more than three years the last year of which he has been employed. If the incapacity of the worker is due to an industrial accident or disease entitling him to the payment of a pension, he can remain in the Member State regardless of the length of his previous residence. If the incapacity did not arise from employment he is entitled to remain if he has resided in the Member State for at least two years.

Worker's Dependants

The principle of non-discrimination must be extended to his or her dependants, otherwise the practical implementation becomes meaningless. This non-discrimination as regards dependants must not be limited to the right to reside in another Member State, together with the worker. It must encompass the whole treatment afforded to national dependants, including education, training, welfare and housing.

Directive 68/360 states that members of the family, irrespective of nationality, have the right to "install" themselves with a worker who is a national of one of the Member State employed in the territory of another.

Under Art.10(1) of Regulation 1612/68 the workers family includes:

(a) his spouse and their descendants who are under the age of 21 years or are dependants;

(b) dependant relatives in the ascending line of the worker and his spouse.

In principle members of the family have rights analogous to the rights of the person primarily concerned, *i.e.* entry, residence and exit, together with social security rights. Family rights terminate with the primary rights of the worker and also when a dependant ceases to be a member of the family, *e.g.* divorced spouse or a married child). In Case 59/85 *Netherlands State v Reed* the ECJ held that the term "spouse" included co-habitee. However, this decision was based upon non-discrimination on the part of the State authorities. The Dutch did not discriminate between a spouse or a co-habitee when dealing with their own nationals and therefore they could not do so in Reed's case. However, if like the UK the host Member State did not treat the spouse and co-habitee alike the decision in *Reed* would not assist them.

The death of the holder of primary rights will not deprive members of his family of their right to remain in the country. If not already acquired the workers survivors will do so if:

(a) resided continuously in the host country for two years preceding his death, or

(b) the worker died from an occupational disease or an industrial accident, or

(c) the surviving spouse was a national of the host country and lost that nationality on marriage to him.

Freedom of movement could nevertheless be illusory if by moving from one MS to another the worker would lose the rights acquired under social security regulations, notably with regards to the pension rights of the worker and his dependants.

The Treaty has therefore provided for the adoption of a system ensuring that

(a) all periods are taken into account under the laws of the several countries where the beneficiary has worked will be added together for calculating the amount of his benefits, and

(b) that those benefits will be paid to the beneficiary in whichever Member State he resides.

Overall, therefore, the freedom of movement for the worker means applying the same treatment to the migrant worker and dependants as to the nationals of the MS of residence.

Obstacles to the Free Movement of Workers

1. Discrimination based on nationality.
2. Incompatibility of the various social security systems.
3. Recognition of educational/professional qualifications.

Therefore any discrimination based on nationality between workers of the Member States as regards employment, renumeration and other labour conditions must be abolished. The workers rights include:

(a) to accept offers of employment actually made;
(b) to move freely within the territory of a Member State for this purpose;
(c) to enter into and reside in a Member State for the purpose of employment in accordance with the provisions governing the employment of nationals of that Member State laid down by law, regulation or administrative action;
(d) to remain in the territory of a Member State after having been employed in that state.

Public Service Employment

The principle of non-discrimination does not apply to employment in the public service Art.39(4) EC (ex 48(4) EC) states, which means that public authorities may refuse to hire non-nationals, but they have to justify such exclusion (Case 137/80 *Commission v Belgium*). The Court has held that the exemption provided by Art.39(4) EC (ex 48(4) EC) does not apply to all employment in the public sector as this is too wide an interpretation. Art.39(4) EC (ex 48(4) EC) applies to those activities in the public service which were connected with the exercise of discretion or official authority involving the national interest. However, once a worker from another Member State is employed in the public service, he must be treated in the same way as the nationals, since exception only concerns access to the post (Case 152/73 *Sotgiu v Deutsche Bundespost*).

Limitations to the Free Movement of Workers

The limitations are specified in Art.39(3) EC (ex 48(3) EC) are on the grounds of Public Policy, Public Security or Public Health. National authorities applying these provisions upon a Community national must justify their action. They cannot impose restrictions upon a Community national unless "his presence or conduct constitutes a genuine and sufficiently serious threat to public policy"—(see Case 36/75 *Roland Rutili v Ministre de l'interieur*). This cannot be applied to a group, but only to individual members of the group (see Case 41/74 *Van Duyn v Home Office*. Directive 64/221 states that it must be "personal conduct". On the basis of the UK government's view of the Church of Scientology, the Court held in *Van Duyn* that the UK's action was justified. The question was asked "Was it discriminatory in that a UK national could have taken up the post Van Duyn had accepted?" The Court response was:

> "a Member State for reasons of public policy, can where it deems necessary, refuse a national of another Member State the benefit of the principle of freedom of movement of workers in a case where such a national proposes to take up a particular offer of employment even though the Member State does not place a similar restriction on its own nationals".

It follows from the case law of the Court that Member States have not relinquished all control over Community nationals as regulations governing the registration of aliens and criminal sanctions in this respect are compatible with their Treaty obligations unless they are so rigorous as to be tantamount to a denial of the freedom of movement over and above the cases covered by the derogation provisions.

Public Policy provides a Member State with discretion but only within the limits allowed for by the Treaty, which are narrowly interpreted by the ECJ. Criminal conviction does not automatically justify deportation. (See Case 67/74 *Bonsignore v Stadt Koln*). In Case 30/77 *R. v Bouchereau* a conviction for drug offences was regarded as a sufficient ground for deportation.

9. THE FREEDOM OF ESTABLISHMENT AND THE FREEDOM TO PROVIDE SERVICES

FREEDOM OF ESTABLISHMENT

Arts 43–48 EC (ex 52–58 EC)

The right of establishment, necessary to exercise a profession or to render a service, is not confined to individuals. It is available to companies and bodies corporate which are treated like individuals. The immigration rules are broadly like those that apply to "workers", but the full enjoyment of "the right of establishment" depends upon the recognition of professional qualifications and this, in turn, depends upon the progress of harmonisation of national laws in this field.

There is no definition of the group of persons entitled to the right of establishment. In distinction from "workers" (who are salaried) Art.43 EC (ex 52 EC) contemplates a group of people who, in principle, pursue activities as self-employed persons or set up and manage undertakings within the meaning of Art.48 EC (ex 58 EC).

Such persons belong, as a rule, to recognised professions whose status and membership is regulated by law. Hence the need of harmonising the national rules and regulations to facilitate their mobility within the Community and, in the first place, to remove restrictions on the ground of nationality and other peculiar national grounds. (See Case 213/89 *R. v Secretary of State for Transport, Ex p. Factortame*).

To carry out its mandate the Council adopted in 1962 two General Programmes for the

(i) Abolition of Restrictions on Freedom to provide Services and
(ii) on Freedom of Establishments,

and in subsequent years has embarked on extensive legislation in these fields. However, as the Commission recorded in its White Paper on completing the internal market, the results as of 1987 were still unsatisfactory. Therefore the Commission recommended action in specific areas including a more efficient policing and enforcement system, resulting in measures to suspend the enforcement of any national legislation which manifestly infringes Community law.

Independently of this harmonisation policy, the ECJ was able to remove some of the restrictions in accordance with the principle of non-discrimination. Thus it has held that a Dutch national resident in Belgium with the appropriate qualifications to practice law could not be debarred from his professional activity on the ground that, according to Belgian law, a lawyer must be a Belgian national (Case 2/74 *Reyners v Belgian State*). Similarly the Court ruled in the case of a Belgian lawyer (Case 71/76 *Thieffry v Conseil de l'Ordre des Avocats a la Cour de Paris*) and a British architect qualified to practise in France (Case 11/77 *Patrick v Ministere des Affaires Culturelles*), a Dutch motor insurance claims investigator in Italy (Case 90/76 *Van Ameyde v UCI*.

The principle of non-discrimination on the ground of nationality was further extended when the Court held that residential qualification of a properly qualified person, was not a legitimate condition of his exercising the profession.

However, conviction for the illegal exercise of the veterinary profession was upheld in the case of a person qualified in Italy who, having become naturalised in France, attempted to practise on his own without first obtaining the requisite French qualifications. Such a bar was considered justified pending the implementation of the harmonising directives (Case 136/78 *Ministere Public v Auer*) but no longer after. In the recent Case 55/94 *Reinhard Gebhard v Consiglio dell'Ordine degli Avvocati e Procuratori di Milano*, the ECJ brought the rules relating to establishment into line with those relating to services.

In the absence of a Treaty definition of the class of persons entitled to the right of establishment was, and is likely to be, confronted with fringe "professions" including sports activities. (Case 36/74 *Walgrave and Koch v Association Union Cycliste Internationale*). So far the Court has held that such activities may come under the non-discrimination principle if they entail "economic activities". Amateur activities seem unaffected by Community rules. In Case 415/93 *Bosman* the ECJ held that Art.48 EC can in certain circumstances impose obligations on individual football clubs and associations not to impose restrictions on the free movement of footballers.

FREEDOM TO PROVIDE SERVICES

Arts 49–55 EC (ex 59–66 EC)

According to Art.50 EC (ex 60 EC) services mean "services for remuneration in particular activities of an industrial and commercial character, craftsmanship and exercise of a profession". However the provision of services is often connected with the exercise of a profession and in this respect inseparable from the right of establishment. The difference between the provision of services and that of establishment is that the latter is associated with actually setting up in another Member State whereas the former involves only a transient visit to provide the services.

Right to Receive Services

Although Arts 49 and 50 EC (ex 59 and 60 EC) provide for the removal of restrictions on the freedom to provide services on the basis of Directive 73/148, they have been interpreted by the European Court of Justice to embrace the freedom to receive services. In Joined Cases 286/82 and 26/83 *Luisi v Ministero del Tesoro*, following the Commission's view in Case 118/75 *Criminal Proceedings Against Watson and Belman*, the Court held that there was a freedom for the recipient of services to go to another Member State, without restriction, in order to receive a service there. Although the case involved the transfer of money out of Italy in breach of Italian currency law for the purpose of tourism and medical treatment, the principle in the judgment included persons travelling for the purpose of education. The right of residence exists during the period for which the service is provided. Any breach of this freedom would be *prima facie* a breach of Arts 49 and 50 EC (ex 59 and 60 EC). (See *R. v Secretary of State for the Home Department, Ex p. Flynn* [1997] 3 C.M.L.R. 888). Directive 93/96 deals specifically with the situation where a student moves to another Member State to undertake a vocational course.

The student, spouse and dependent children have the right to remain for the duration of the course. The right does not generally apply to a co-habitee (Case 59/85 *Netherlands State v Reed*). In every case the student must assure the relevant national authority that he has sufficient resources to avoid becoming a burden on the social assistance system of the host Member State during the period of residence.

Vocational Training

The Court has given a wide definition to the meaning of vocational education. In Case 29/83 *Gravier v City of Liege* the Court held it to include all forms of teaching which prepares for and leads directly to a particular profession or which provides the necessary skills for such a profession. In these circumstances a student may claim equal access and on the same basis as nationals of the Member State. This was confirmed in Case 24/86 *Blaizot v University of Liege*, where the course involved was a university veterinary studies course.

Derogation

As with all the freedoms arising from the Treaty there are exceptions where the Member State may derogate from their obligation under the Treaty. These are specifically those in Arts 46 and 55 EC (ex 56 and 66 EC), which allow for derogation on the grounds of public policy, public security and public health. The public policy provision has been interpreted strictly by the European Court to ensure that its scope is not unilaterally determined by a Member State without control by the European Community institutions (*Van Duyn*). In Case 36/75 *Rutili v Ministre de l'Interieur* the Court held that restrictions on the movement of an EC national on the grounds of public policy could only be accepted where the behaviour of the individual constitutes a genuine and sufficiently serious threat to public policy.

Directive 64/221

Art.3(1) of Directive 64/221 states that any exclusion on the grounds of public policy or public security must be based exclusively on the personal conduct of the individual. In *Van Duyn* the Court held that although past association with an organisation does not count as personal conduct, present association does and the activities in question must constitute a genuine and sufficiently serious threat to public policy affecting one of the fundamental interests of society. In this case the Court allowed the UK to apply a stricter standard on an EC national than the one it applied to its own nationals because the UK deemed that it was necessary. In *Bonsignore* it was accepted that the concept of personal conduct expresses the requirement that a deportation order may only be made for breaches of the peace and public security which might be committed by the individual concerned.

Under Art.6 of Directive 64/221 the individual is entitled to know on which ground, *i.e.* public policy or public security, the decision is based, unless this information contravenes state security. This allows the individual to prepare his defence. If a Member State fails to comply with Art.6 it may lead to the quashing of a deportation order (*R. v Secretary of State for the Home Office, Ex p. Dannemberg*). Article 8 of the Directive requires that the individual is entitled to the same legal remedies in relation to a decision on entry as any other national. For example in the UK an immigrant normally has a right of appeal against immigration decisions to a person called an adjudicator and then to the Immigration Appeal Tribunal. Such appeals cover issues of fact, law and the exercise of discretion, so the merits of the decision would be fully reviewed.

Mutual Recognition

The European Community principle of equal treatment is not always sufficient to ensure that the immigrant is able to practice his profession in another Member State. There is no directly applicable provision in the EC Treaty requiring Member States to recognise qualifications acquired in another Member State or obliging them to allow immigrants to practice a profession without the appropriate qualifications (Case 136/78 *Ministere Public v Auer*).

In order to make the right of establishment effective the Community embarked on a harmonising process in which the rules governing the formation and exercise of the medical profession took the lead. Article 47(1) EC (ex 57(1) EC) requires the Council to adopt directives on the mutual recognition of diplomas, certificates and other evidence of formal qualifications. Without a relevant directive the migrant is likely to find that Community law is of limited assistance to him. The Commission had attempted to remedy the situation by promoting separate directives for each profession, such as medicine, dentistry, veterinary medicine, midwifery and the exercise of the profession of architect. The objective of these directives has been to make it easier for a person practising a profession in one Member State to practice that profession in another Member State.

However, in order to avoid legislating piecemeal the Mutual Recognition Directive 89/48 was adopted. Like all directives on establishment Directive 89/48 benefits Community citizens with regard to qualifications awarded in a Member State. Under this Directive recognition is to be given to diplomas as defined by Art.1(a). There must be three essential characteristics for such "diplomas"; it must be awarded by a competent authority in a Member State following the successful completion of a course lasting at least three years at a university or equivalent institution plus professional training. Finally such a "diploma" must qualify the holder for the pursuit of a regulated profession in a Member State. Article 3 of the Directive provides the basic rule that if a Member State requires a "diploma" as a condition for exercising a regulated profession, it must accept a "diploma" obtained in another Member State.

Lawyers

The Commission had attempted to deal with various professional bodies by promoting separate directives for each. The objective of these directives has been to make it easier for a person practising a profession in one Member State to practice that profession in another Member State. However, the important difference between these professions and lawyers is that although the principles of medicine or dentistry are much the same in every Member State, those of law differ. It is therefore hardly surprising that the progress on facilitating the free movement of lawyers has been very slow.

Directive 77/249 was specifically aimed at lawyer's but it is only concerned with the provision of services and not the right of establishment. It makes provision for lawyer's to carry out their profession in another Member State on a temporary basis. Lawyer under this Directive is defined by a list of terms to reflect the diversity in the European Community. The function of the list is to indicate those practitioners who are able to benefit from the rights conferred by the Directive and the activities to which it applies. Thus anyone who is recognised as a "lawyer" for the purpose of the Directive can perform the work of a lawyer in another Member State but only on a temporary basis. While he is performing this work he must use the title of his home country, as it would appear in that country. In this capacity the foreign lawyer can do all the work of a local lawyer, unless the national law of the Member State reserves certain activities for its national lawyers and on the proviso that he represents a client in court work in conjunction with a local lawyer. In the UK such foreign lawyers can not undertake probate or conveyancing work, which is reserved for UK lawyers.

The Mutual Recognition Directive 89/48 discussed above applies to the legal profession. The profession of a lawyer is in the list of regulated professions. Article 3 of the Directive provides the basic rule that if a Member State requires a "diploma" as a condition for exercising a regulated profession, it must accept a "diploma" obtained in another Member State. In contrast to the situation where a lawyer is providing a "service" of a temporary nature, when he is exercising the right of establishment the lawyer is entitled to use the professional designation of the Member State in which he practices. Thus a French avocat who establishes himself and practices in the UK can call himself a solicitor.

The Directive does recognise that professional training does vary between Member States and allows the Member State where the individual wishes to practice to set certain conditions. This may involve an adaptation period during which super-vision by a qualified practitioner is required of the foreign national or an aptitude test of professional knowledge. In England the test for foreign lawyers wishing to practice as solicitors is called the Qualified Lawyers Transfer Test. Having successfully passed this test the normal rules concerning regis-tration and admission to the appropriate professional body will apply.

Companies

The EC Treaty identifies two rights for companies, namely establishment and provision of services. Under Art.43 EC (ex 52 EC) companies have the right to establish themselves in another Member State by setting up agencies, branches or subsidiaries. Having so established themselves, the companies have the right not to be discriminated against and must be treated under the same conditions as those laid down by the Member State for its own nationals. The same rule applies to companies as it does to individuals, who must be national's of a Member State if they are to benefit from the freedom specified in the Treaty. Article 48(1) EC (ex 58(1) EC) specifies that as far as companies are concerned they must be formed in accordance with the law of a

Member State and have their registered office, central administration or principal place of business within the Community. The Court of Justice held in Case 79/85 *Segers* that to allow a Member State in which a company carried on its business to treat that company in a different manner solely because its registered office was in another Member State would render Art.48 EC (ex 58 EC) valueless. This was confirmed by the ECJ in Case 212/97 *Centros Ltd*, which involved an attempt by the Danish Trade and Companies Board to refuse to register a company set up, but not trading, in England.

Just as there is a requirement that workers and the self-employed should receive remuneration in order to satisfy the Treaty, so companies which are non-profit making do not come within the definition of Art.48(1) EC (ex 58(1) EC). The remuneration requirement is repeated in Art.49 EC (ex 59 EC) dealing with the right to provide services. This provision deals with a company established in one Member State providing service of an industrial, commercial or professional nature in another Member State. The main difference with services is that in contrast to establishment the company is entering another Member State only temporarily to pursue this activity.

Article 293 EC (ex 220 EC) requires the Member States to negotiate conventions with each other in order to secure uniformity of recognition of business practices across the Community. The article specifically mentions the mutual recognition of companies within the meaning of Art.48(2) EC (ex 58(2) EC). As a result of this requirement a Convention on the Mutual Recognition of Companies and Bodies Corporate was signed in 1968 by the six founder members of the European Community. However, it is not in force as it was not ratified by the Member State. Given this failure but recognising the importance of company law, the policy of the EC has been to move forward on the basis of directives dealing with specific matters. The fact that over thirteen directives have been proposed reflects the extensive programme of harmonisation of company law embarked upon by the European Community. Although not all of these directives have been adopted, those which have cover such technical matters as company capital, company accounts, appointment of auditors and disclosure of information. These are important because companies established or providing services in different Member States facing the need to adjust to different regulatory regimes may lead to duplication of accounting, licensing and other requirements. This would act as a disincentive to penetrating other national markets. It may also reduce the opportunities for benefiting from economies of scale.

Another way of seeking to reduce the problems for companies operating in more than one Member State is to establish EC corporate structures. The first step was taken in this development with the establishment of European Economic Interest Grouping by Regulation 2173/85. These EEIGs permit companies and others to co-operate within the Community on a cross-border basis, and thus provide a vehicle for joint ventures. EEIGs have the mixed characteristics of companies and partnership. They are not separate in the sense that the companies are still liable for the debts of the EEIG but they do have a separate legal capacity. Such Groups have to be registered, which in the UK is a requirement to register with the Registrar of Companies. An EEIG cannot have more than 500 employees or offer any share participation to the public. Obviously there are certain limitations with EEIG but they do provide a flexible vehicle for economic activity.

The ultimate aim of the Community is to have a new company formation which will have legal capacity throughout the Community. This is to be the European Company or *Societas Europaea* (SE) which will be established by registration with the European Court in Luxembourg under a distinctive European Community company statute. Even though registration would be with the Court, the SE would be domiciled in a particular Member State. The intended role of the SE is to facilitate cross-border co-operation by means of large-scale mergers and associations. It can be seen that this is perhaps the natural extension from the EEIG which facilitates such ventures but on a smaller scale. There have been some criticisms of the establishment of SEs which have led to delay in the adoption of the necessary Community legislation. However, the proposal was given a new impetus at the Nice IGC and in October 2001 the Council adopted the Regulation and Directive on the SE which will enter into force in October 2004.

10. SEX DISCRIMINATION

The Treaty Rule

In Pt One of the EC Treaty, where the underlying principles of the Community are listed, reference is made to the principle of equality. This indicates the special status given by Community law to the principle of equality. The specific Article dealing with equality in employment is Art.141 EC (ex 119 EC).

Article 141 EC (ex 119(1)EC) of the Treaty provides that:

> "Each Member State shall during the first (transitional) stage ensure and subsequently maintain the application of the principle that men and women should receive equal pay for equal work."

Pay is defined in Art.141 EC (ex 119(2) EC) as the ordinary basic or minimum wage or salary and any other consideration, whether in cash or in kind, which the worker receives, directly or indirectly, in respect of his employment from his employer.

The term "consideration" should not be interpreted too restrictively as it has been held by the ECJ to include other benefits such as favourable rates for family travel for railway employees (Case 12/81 *Garland v BREL*). As long as the "pay" has been (1) received by the employee in respect of his employment and (2) received from the employer, it will come within the meaning of the Article. Thus it includes pensions paid under a contracted-out private occupational scheme (Case 262/88 *Barber v Guardian Royal Exchange Assurance Group*). See also Case 7/93 *Beune*).

In Case 43/75 *Defrenne v Sabena* the Court of European Justice held that the article has direct effect the Court has identified a right which can be enforced by the individual employee in the courts of the Member State. Madame Defrenne had been employed by the Belgian airline Sabena as an air hostess. She complained of being paid a lower salary than her male colleagues although the work they did was the same. In an Art.234 EC (ex 177 EC) reference the Belgian court asked if Art.141 EC (ex 119 EC) could be relied upon before national courts. In its judgment the court said that discrimination on the grounds of sex could be indirect and disguised discrimination or direct and overt discrimination. The latter type of discrimination was more easily identified and could be based solely upon the criteria of equal work and equal pay referred to in Art.141 EC (ex 119 EC). In such cases Art.141 EC (ex 119 EC) was directly effective and gave use to individual rights which national courts must protect. It was necessary for additional measures to be taken with regard to indirect discrimination. This was achieved by the Equal Pay Directive 75/117 which supplements Art.141 EC (ex 119 EC).

Article 141 EC (ex 119 EC) requires that men and women should receive equal pay for equal work. In Case 129/79 *Macarthys Ltd v Wendy Smith* the Court held that a requirement of contemporaneity of employment is not to be read into the article. Smith was paid £50 per week whereas her male predecessor had received £60. Under UK legislation the requirement was for the male and female workers to be doing the same job at the same time if a comparison was to be made. However, the Court of Justice held that the only issue was whether or not the work was "equal" and it did not matter whether or not the man and woman whose work and pay were to be compared were employed at the same time in the undertaking or not.

In Case 127/92 *Enderby v Frenchay HA* the Court held that the burden of proof, which is normally on the claimant, might shift to the employer where that is necessary to avoid depriving workers who appear to be victims of discrimination of any effective means of enforcing the principle of equal pay.

In Case 170/84 *Bilka-Kaufhaus GmbH v Weber von Harz*, Weber was a female part-time worker who was seeking to challenge her employer's occupational pension scheme. Although the scheme was non-contributory for full-time employees with the employer paying all the contributions, this was not the case with part-timers. Under the scheme, only part-time employees who had been employed by the company for at least 15 out of a total of 20 years could qualify. The Court held that the benefit constituted consideration paid by the employer to the employee in respect of her employment and thus came within Art.141 EC (ex 119 EC). Also in this case the Court provided guidelines to assist in identifying what might constitute objective justification for such differences in pay. The onus is on the employer to prove that the difference in treatment corresponded to a genuine need of the enterprise.

In Case 171/88 *Rinner-Kuhn v FWW Spezial Gebäudereiniging GmbH* Art.141 EC (ex 119 EC) was also held by the Court to be applicable to a statutory social security benefit. This case also included a part-time employee who was employed as a cleaner.

She challenged the German legislation which permitted employers to exclude workers who worked less than ten hours per week from entitlement to sick pay. Despite statements in Case 192/85 *Newstead v Department of Transport* that social security schemes were outside the scope of Art.141 EC (ex 119 EC), the Court held that sick pay fell within the Article. Therefore the German legislation was contrary to Art.141 EC (ex 119 EC). In an action brought by the Equal Opportunities Commission in 1994, the House of Lords held that the qualifying periods of employment in the UK's Employment Protection (Consolidation) Act 1978 were contrary to EC law. This was because they differentiated unfairly between part-time and full-time employees.

In *Barber* a group of male employees challenged their employer's contracted-out pension scheme. The employer's scheme was a substitute for the statutory scheme and was payable at different ages for men and women. The Court held that since the worker received these benefits from his employer as a result of his employment, the fact that the benefits were payable at different ages for men and women resulted in a difference in pay. Following this case it would appear that the only social security pension schemes provided for workers which fall outside the scope of Art.141 EC (ex 119 EC) are those which provide for workers in general, as a matter of social policy.

Following the *Barber* and *Bilko-Kaufhause* cases there have been a number of important developments. In Case 200/91 *Coloroll Pension Trustees Ltd v Russell* it was held that Art.141 EC (ex 119 EC) applied to occupational pension schemes and confirmed that survivors and dependents' benefits constitute pay under the article. In Case 57/93 *Vroege v NCIV Institut voor Volkshuisvesting BV* and Case 128/93 *Fisscher v Stichting Bedrijfspensioenfonds voor de Detailhandel* the exclusion of married women and part-time workers from occupational schemes was also contrary to Art.141 EC (ex 119 EC). However, in Case 249/96 *Grant v South-West Trains Ltd* the ECJ rejected the claim by a female employee with a female partner for rail benefits to which heterosexual couples were entitled. The ECJ stated that references to "sex discrimination" was not a reference to gender orientation. This was confirmed by Case 264/97 *D v Council* where the Court said that it was "unfit" as a judicial institution to bring about a positive change which was properly to be enacted by legislation. However, in *Chief Constable of West*

Yorkshire Police v A the Court of Appeal held that the Equal Treatment Directive covered discrimination against a transsexual.

Directives

The basic role of the EC Treaty has been developed and refined by a number of directives.

Directive 75/117 on equal pay for men and women. Art.1 of this Directive provides for the elimination of all discrimination on the grounds of sex with regard to all aspects and conditions of remuneration. This Directive defined the scope of Art.141 EC (ex 119 EC) and introduced the principle of equal pay for work of equal value. Thus this directive met the points raised by the ECJ in *Defrenne* as to why Art.141 EC (ex 119 EC) could not apply to indirect discrimination. The UK government implemented this Directive by means of the Sex Discrimination Act 1975 but not to the satisfaction of the Commission who brought proceedings under Art.226 EC (ex 169 EC) (see *Commission v UK*). This resulted in the Equal Pay (Amendment) Regulations 1983 which empowered a panel of independent experts to prepare a report on whether or not any work was of equal value to that of a man in the same employment. (See Case 96/80 *Jenkins v Kingsgate (Clothing Productions) Ltd*).

Directive 76/207 on equal treatment for men and women as regards access to employment, vocational training and promotion, and working conditions. The principle of "equal treatment" is defined as meaning "that there shall be no discrimination whatsoever on grounds of sex either directly or indirectly by reference in particular to material or family status". The important case of Case 271/91 *Marshall v Southampton & South West Hampshire AHA* was brought under this Directive. The Court in this case held that the Directive was directly effective as the employer was an emanation of the State (see Chapter 3 above, p.27). In the subsequent Case 271/91 *Marshall v Southampton & South West Hampshire AHA No. 2*, Mrs Marshall successfully challenged the UK legislation which limited the compensation paid to those individuals who had been discriminated against on the grounds of sex.

Directive 79/7 on equal treatment in occupational and social security schemes. This Directive applies to the working population both employed and self-employed and includes those whose work has been interrupted by illness, accident or involuntary unemployment. (Case 208/90 *Emmott v Minister for Social Welfare*). There are exemptions to the principle of equal treatment, *e.g.* the determination of pensionable age for the granting of retirement pensions. This Directive has made little impact upon the various forms of indirect discrimination (see Joined Cases 63/91 & 64/91 *Jackson & Cresswell v Chief Adjudication Officer*).

Directive 86/378 on equal treatment in occupational social security schemes. As "occupational pensions" are to be considered as "pay" under the *Barber* judgment, the importance of this Directive has been reduced.

Directive 86/613 on equal treatment in self-employed occupations. This Directive extends the application of Directive 76/207 to the self-employed.

Directive 92/85 provides a uniform level of social protection for pregnant workers and those who have recently given birth. Under Art.10 of this Directive a pregnant worker, whether full time or part-time, may not be dismissed.

Application of the Sex Discrimination Rules

In response to the *Barber* case and its implications for employers and pension funds, a Protocol was annexed to the TEU to limit its impact. It states that

> "For the purpose of Article 141 EC (ex 119 EC) of the Treaty . . ., benefits under occupational social security schemes shall not be considered as remunerations if and in so far as they are attributable to periods of employment prior to May 17, 1990, except in the case of workers or those claiming under them who have before that date initiated legal proceedings or introduced an equivalent claim under the applicable national law."

In addition the Protocol on Social Policy added by Art.6 of the Agreement attached to it, purports to permit a Member State to maintain or adopt measures discriminating in favour of women in certain circumstances. The precise meaning of this is unclear, especially as the UK explicitly excludes itself from this Protocol. In *Dekker* the ECJ held that refusal to employ a woman because she was pregnant was *per se* direct discrimination on grounds of sex under Art.2(1) of the Equal Treatment Directive. As pregnancy was something which could only happen to a woman, refusal to employ because of Dekker's pregnancy was direct discrimination. Similarly in Case 179/88 *Handels-og Kontorfunktionaerernes Forbund v Dansk Arbejdsgiverforening* (the *Hertz* case) the dismissal of a woman because of her pregnancy was ruled by the Court to be direct discrimination. If there had been another reason for the dismissal, such as absence from work through illness originating in pregnancy this would not be direct discrimination. In Case 32/93 *Webb v EMO Air Cargo (UK) Ltd* the ECJ reaffirmed that dismissal for reasons of pregnancy is illegal.

11. THE TREATY ON EUROPEAN UNION AND BEYOND

The Treaty on European Union (TEU) was signed in Maastricht on February 7, 1992 and came into force on November 1, 1993. This was later than anticipated by Art.52 TEU (ex R(2)) due to delays in ratification caused by referendum in Ireland, France and Denmark and legal action in the UK and Germany. For the first time it became legally correct to refer to the European Community since this is the new name under Art.8 TEU (ex G(1)) for the European Economic Community. The word economic has been dropped to reflect the fact that there has been a change of emphasis towards non-economic provisions such as citizenship.

The TEU was the result of two regulation conferences, one on political union and the other relating to economic and monetary union. The TEU articles were numbered alphabetically to avoid confusion with the founding treaties which it amended. The result was that the treaties of the Community were lengthy documents and quite complex. The Treaty of Amsterdam has resolved this by completely renumbering the EC and EU treaties, which is why both the old and new article numbers are given in this book so as to avoid confusion.

Treaty of Amsterdam

The original TEU signed at Maastricht was to be reconsidered at an intergovernmental conference (IGC) in 1996/1997. At the IGC held in Amsterdam in 1997 the governments of the Member States negotiated about the changes to the TEU. The Treaty of Amsterdam came into effect on May 1, 1999. The main pressures on the negotiations were:

1. As indicated above, some Member States experienced problems in ratifying the Maastricht Treaty due to the feeling that the EU was not relevant or accountable to ordinary people. The Treaty of Amsterdam attempts to deal with this by emphasising employment within the Union (see Art.2 TEU and Title VIII EC). Reference is also made to sustainable development with regard to protecting the environment.

2. Applications had been received from ten former central and eastern European states plus Turkey and Cyprus for membership of the Union. This potential enlargement of the Union could not be accomplished within the present institutional structure.

The changes to the institutions are dealt with in Chapter 1 above, p.1, but there are some others which will not come into operation until there has been enlargement to 20 Member States. In relation to the European Parliament the number of MEPs has been fixed at 700 regardless of the number of states, although this has now been increased to 732 by the Treaty of Nice. Therefore, there will need to be some reallocation of seats to accommodate new members of the Union. The European Commission will also be affected by making it one Commissioner per Member State, thus removing the extra Commissioner enjoyed by the UK, Germany, France, Italy and Spain. As far as the Council of Ministers is concerned there will be more emphasis on qualified majority voting (QMV).

Main points from the amended TEU

Acquis Communautaire Article 2 TEU (ex Article B) explicitly refers to *acquis communautaire*, a principle which had been previously associated with the accession of new Member States. There is no formal definition of the term but it goes beyond the formal acceptance of Community law to include rules which have no binding force. These would include recommendations and opinions of the Council and Commission, resolutions of the Council and common agreements of the Member States. Some writers believe that the term has more of a political than a legal meaning. Perhaps the development of the Community into the fields of co-operation in foreign policy, Justice and Home Affairs measures has brought about the need to ensure that Member States work closely together. How it will work in practice will become clearer as the Community acts on these policies.

Subsidiarity   Article 5 EC (ex 3(b) EC) now states that:

> "the Community shall take action, in accordance with the principle of subsidiarity, only if and in so far as the objectives of the proposed action cannot be sufficiently achieved by the Member States and can therefore by reason of the scale or effects of the proposed action, be better achieved by the Community".

This article follows the statements in the Preamble that:

> "the process of creating an ever closer union among the peoples of Europe in which decisions are taken as closely as possible to the citizens in accordance with the principle of subsidiarity".

As it is the European Commission which makes proposals, it would appear that the onus is on it to justify its action at Community level rather than leaving it to the Member States. This could perhaps lend to a challenge in the European Court of Justice on the grounds that the proposed Community measure offends against the principle of subsidiarity. The Treaty of Amsterdam has a Protocol on the application of the Principles of Subsidiarity and Proportionality. This builds upon the guidelines developed in recent years and gives them the force of law. The Protocol cites three criteria for judging whether the conditions have been fulfilled:

1. Does the action have transnational aspects that cannot be satisfactorily regulated by the Member States?
2. Would action by the Member States or lack of action conflict with the requirements of the Treaty?
3. Would action at Community level produce clear benefits?

Amendments to the EC Treaty

1. Change in name. The term economic is dropped, as the Community is now to be known as the European Community (Art.8 TEU). This change acknowledges the reality

of today when Community competence is no longer restricted to the economic domain. The areas of activity in the amended Art.5 EC (ex 3 EC) show extension to citizenship, social cohesion and social development and the environment.

2. Article 1 TEU states that the Union is "founded on" the Communities, supplemented by the policies and forms of co-operation established by the TEU. Unlike the European Community under Art.281 EC (ex 210 EC), the new Union does not have legal personality. Article 5 TEU (ex E TEU) makes it clear that the Union operates under or through the institutions of the Community. However, the objectives of the Union are wider than those of the EC, notably in the fields of foreign and security policy and justice and home affairs.

3. Article 6 (2) TEU (ex F(2) TEU) requires the Union to respect fundamental rights, both as guaranteed by the European Convention on Human Rights and Fundamental Freedoms and as they result from the constitutional traditions common to the Member States. This Article repeats much of the language used by the ECJ in its case law relating to the protection of fundamental rights as a general principle of Community law.

4. Article 7 TEU (ex F(1) TEU) requires the Union to respect the national identities of its Member States. This idea complements the principle of subsidiarity (Art.5 EC) but also includes the cultural heritage of the Member States. It also recognises that the system of government found in all Member States is based on the principles of democracy.

   The Treaty of Amsterdam includes a Protocol which encourages closer ties with the national parliaments of Member States. There is to be a six week interval between the tabling of any legislative proposal and appearance on the Council agenda. This will give national parliaments an opportunity to hold a debate and thus contribute to wider discussion of legislative proposals.

5. The European Community is to conduct its activities on the basis of "an open market economy with free competition".

Citizenship of the Union

The TEU contained five new Articles 17–21 EC (ex 8 to 8(d) EC), concerning citizenship of the Union. Although citizenship of the

Union is established, the rights conferred and the duties imposed are those which flow from the EC Treaty. This is because the main impact is by the amendments the TEU makes to the EC Treaty and not as an independent Treaty. These do not materially affect the existing rights of economically active persons (see free movement of workers and the right of establishment above, pp.79–86).

Citizenship of the Union is mandatory for all nationals of the Member States, there is no provision for opting out. However, the Treaty of Amsterdam has amended the EC Treaty to reflect the point that citizenship of the Europe Union will complement and not replace national citizenship. All Union citizens residing in a Member State of which he or she is not a national has the right to vote and stand as a candidate in both municipal elections and elections to the European Parliament in that State.

If the Union citizen is in a third country where the Member State of which he is a national is not represented, he is entitled to protection by the diplomatic authorities of any Member State, on the same conditions as that State's own nationals. There is also the right to petition the EP and to apply to the Ombudsman who was appointed by the Parliament in 1996 under Arts 21 EC (ex 8(d) EC), 194 EC (ex 138(d)) and 195 EC (ex 138(e)). The Ombudsman has wide-ranging powers of inquiry and can request documents and evidence from Community institutions. He is empowered to act as a conciliator between citizens and the Community administration and can, if appropriate, refer a case to the EP. Every citizen of the Union has the right to write to the EU institutions, including the Ombudsman, in their own language and to receive a reply in their own language, which is assumed to be one of the 12 official languages.

Three Pillars

The TEU makes the point that the Community is built on three pillars, like a temple. The first pillar is the European Community as it now exists, the second refers to home affairs and justice, and the third to a common foreign and security policy. It should be noted that these two latter areas of policy are inter-governmental bodies and are not covered by the voting procedures in the Council of Ministers or as binding on Member States as other areas of EC Treaty policy. However, with the Treaty requirement for Member States to work together within a common position the decisions of these inter-governmental bodies are important. The European Commission is associated with the work of these bodies and the European Parliament is kept informed.

The home affairs and justice policy includes policies on asylum, drugs, refugees and terrorism.

It is claimed that with the completion of the internal market and the removal of border controls, there has to be common European Community approach to these problems. The co-operation on justice and home affairs introduced by the Maastricht Treaty is to be incorporated into the Community by the creation of an "area for freedom, security and justice" by the Treaty of Amsterdam. This will be achieved over a period of five years, although under specific protocols the UK, Ireland and Demark are excluded from this development. The object is to make it easier for European citizens and nationals of non-member countries to move freely, while at the same time building up effective co-operation on border controls, asylum and immigration matters and the fight against international crime. This has been achieved by the incorporation of the Schengen Convention 1990 into the EC Treaty. Thus only police and judicial co-operation will remain under the third pillar, but to which the Treaty of Amsterdam now adds "preventing and combatting of racism and xenophobia".

A common foreign and security policy (CFSP) was in its infancy in the original TEU and the Commission and the Council wished to establish the machinery for "joint action". The reality of the post-Yugoslavia disintegration showed that this needed amendment, with the aim of providing an effective and coherent external policy. The Treaty of Amsterdam introduced more efficient decision making based on qualified majority voting and the safeguard of "constructive abstention". This is designed to improve the ability of the EU to defend its interest on the international stage. The post of High Representative for the common foreign and security policy has been created to resolve some of the problems with the CFSP by providing continuity. Lastly, the common commercial policy is also extended to include services and intellectual property rights in the new Art.133 EC. This will help in negotiations within the World Trade Organisation.

Treaty of Nice

The IGC at Nice in 2000 led to the Treaty of Nice being approved in February 2001. Although there had been problems in ratification in Ireland these have been resolved. The Irish government held a referendum in June 2001, as required by the Irish constitution, but this resulted in a "no" majority. However, in October 2002 another referendum provided a positive response to the Treaty of Nice. Therefore all Member States had ratified the Treaty by the end of October 2002.

The main emphasis of the Treaty of Nice is to prepare the way for the enlargement of the EU. In 2004 the number of Member States will increase to 25 and in 2007 it will be 27. As the result of the political reluctance to grapple with the problem, the institutions have remained largely the same since the time when there were only six Member States. The impending enlargement concentrated the minds of those heads of government meeting at Nice.

Main implications for the EU institutions arising from the Treaty of Nice:

1. *The European Parliament*—As a result of the decision to cap the number of MEPs to 732 on enlargement of the existing Member States, with the exception of Germany and Luxembourg, have had the number of elected representatives reduced.

2. *The Council of Ministers*—From January 1 the system of decision by qualified majority voting will be modified. This will mean that in future a qualified majority will be secured when the number of votes in favour is close to the present threshold of 71 per cent and the majority of Member States vote in favour. In addition a Member State may ask for verification that the qualified majority comprises at least 62 per cent of the total population of the EU. If this is not the case the measure will not be adopted. The policy areas requiring qualified majority voting were also extended.

3. *Co-decision Procedure*—In order for the EU to become more democratic those policy areas that were now to be subject to qualified majority voting in the Council would also give more authority to the European Parliament by making them subject to the co-decision procedure.

4. *The Commission*—From 2005 onwards the Commission will consist of one Commissioner per Member State. When there are 27 Member States the number of Commissioners will not be one per State, but will be on a rotation system based on the principle of equality. The President of the Commission has also been given greater authority

to organise the internal administration of the Commission and can request a Commissioner to resign if he has the support of the remainder of the Commissioners to do so.

5. *The Court of Justice*—With the increasing case load and resulting delays for cases to be heard the impending enlargement would only make this worse, even with the increased number of judges. Therefore, to ease the workload of the Court of Justice the Court of First Instance will be taking requests for preliminary rulings in certain specific areas. For the latter's workload to be reduced there will be a number of specialist chambers to take over the jurisdiction for staff cases and possibly some aspects of intellectual property.

6. *Closer Co-operation*—Some believe that this will lead to a two-speed Community but the Treaty of Amsterdam allowed for the possibility for a number of Member States to establish a closer co-operation between themselves but within the framework of the Treaty. The Treaty of Nice has extended this within the second pillar of common foreign and security policy. A minimum of eight Member States is needed to form a closer co-operation. The veto mechanism to stop this closer co-operation has been abolished as each Member State now has the right to refer the matter to the European Council. If the matter comes within the EC pillar of the EU the European Parliament must give its assent to the development.

Convention on the Future of Europe

At Nice there was a "Declaration on the Future of the Union", which was followed up in December 2001 by the Laeken Declaration. The result was that the European Council decided to convene a Convention on the Future of Europe. The task of this Convention is to consider the key issues arising from the EU's future development and to try to identify the various possible responses. The membership of the Convention is drawn from the EU institutions and the national parliaments and governments. It is likely that the next IGC in 2004 will discuss the report from the Convention and consider any necessary changes to the treaties.

12. THE EUROPEAN CONVENTION ON HUMAN RIGHTS

There is always confusion about the relationship between the EU and the European Law dealing with human rights. The media often compound the problem by referring to the European Court without recording the fact that they are referring to the court adjudicating on this convention and not the European Court of Justice of the EU. This chapter is intended to clarify the distinction.

Following the atrocities of the Second World War, there was an impetus for an agreement directed at protecting the individual rights of people in Europe. The European Convention on Human Rights was drafted in 1949 and was influenced by the UN Declaration of Human Rights adopted in 1948. It has been extended by a number of protocols since then. All the Member States of the EU are parties to the Convention.

The UK was a signatory to the Convention in 1950 and it came into force in 1953. The Convention is binding in international law. However, some legal systems treat international law differently from national or domestic law, *i.e.* depending upon whether a Dualist or Monist approach is taken (see Chapter 3, p.29). Thus the UK, as a dualist system, had to specifically legislate with the Human Rights Act 1998 to make the Convention available in UK courts.

Human Rights Machinery

The original human rights machinery consisted of the Commission of Human Rights, which received and examined complaints about the infringement of human rights, and the European Court of Human Rights, which adjudicated on cases which were referred to it by the Commission. There is also the Committee of Ministers of the Council of Europe, which consists of the Foreign Ministers of the High Contracting Parties.

The increasing case-load prompted a reform of the Convention supervisory machinery. The outcome of the debate was the decision to abolish the Commission and create a single full-time Court. This Court is composed of 41 judges, which is equivalent to the number of Contracting States. The judges are elected by the Parliamentary Assembly of the Council of Europe for a term of six years, with half retiring every three years. The judges sit on the Court in their individual capacity and do not represent any State. Committees of three judges sit to carry out the filtering work formerly carried out by the Commission. The Court sits in chambers of seven judges, although in exceptional circumstances it may sit as a Grand Chamber consisting of 17. Where the Court finds that there has been a breach of the Convention, it has the power to order the offending State to make just compensation. If changes are necessary to domestic legislation, the offending state is free to determine what these should be in order to comply with its obligations under the Convention.

RIGHT OF INDIVIDUAL PETITION

Although initially the purpose of the Convention was directed at preventing large scale infringements of human rights by States which were party to it, the right of individual petition became effective on July 5, 1955. The UK recognised the right of individual petition in 1966. It is this right of individual petition that has given rise to the bulk of the cases coming before the Commission. This change of emphasis has led to the Convention being seen as a bulwark against specific infringements of human rights rather than large scale violations.

Applications can be admitted from individual persons, non-governmental organisations or groups of individuals provided that the alleged violation concerns them directly. The application can only be brought against a Contracting Party to the Convention, *i.e.* a government or its agents. They can not be brought against private individuals or bodies whose acts do not entail the responsibility of a Contracting Party.

As a "dualist" system the Convention did not become part of domestic law within the UK when the UK signed the Convention. However, as with other international treaty obligations, the Convention was applicable in the interpretation of statute law. This is based on the generally recognised principle of construction that Parliament does not intend to legislate contrary to the UK's international obligations. The House of Lords has indicated that where the law is either unclear or ambiguous, or concerns an issue not yet ruled on, the courts ought to consider the implications of the Convention (*Derbyshire CC v Times Newspapers Ltd* [1992] 3 W.L.R. 28). However, this situation has been superseded by the Human Rights Act 1998.

Human Rights Act 1998

The aim of introducing the Human Rights Act 1998 (HRA) is to make more directly accessible the rights which the British people already enjoy under the European Convention on Human Rights. The Act will thus obviate the need to take human rights issues to Strasbourg.

Section 2 of the HRA requires courts and tribunals to take into account the "Strasbourg jurisprudence", *i.e.* previous decisions of the European Human Rights Court or the European Commission on Human Rights before its abolition. However, it is not just the courts and tribunals which will be affected, as the Act requires a whole new culture to be developed by public authorities and government bodies. Section 3(1) states that "so far as it is possible to do so, primary legislation must be read and given effect in a way which is compatible with the Convention rights". It is no wonder that the implementation date for the Act has been put back to allow public bodies, government departments and the courts to review their procedures and train their staff.

Section 8(1) gives the courts wide powers, including the award of damages to injured parties:

> "In relation to any act (or proposed act) of a public authority which the court finds is (or would be) unlawful, it may grant such relief or remedy, or make such order, within its powers as it considers just and appropriate".

The Convention and the EU

In 1976 the Commission ruled out the necessity of accession by the Community to the Convention, but it did call for a joint declaration by the three political institutions affirming their commitment to fundamental rights. This Joint Declaration was made in 1977. However, in 1979 the Commission did formally propose accession to the Council and subsequently the European Parliament made statements supporting this development. However, the ECJ in its Opinion No.2/94 stated that as Community law stood the EC had no competence to accede to the Convention. In its Opinion the ECJ pointed out that although the original treaties made no specific mention of fundamental rights, the Court had in its judgments upheld the protection by way of general principles of Community law. Specific mention has also been made of the Convention in the Preamble to both the Single European Act and the Treaty on European Union. This has been repeated in the Treaty of Amsterdam which amends Art.6 TEU so as to reaffirm the principle of respect for human rights and fundamental freedoms. There is also the Charter of Fundamental Rights of the European Union, agreed at the Nice IGC, but which does not at present have legal force. It reaffirms the commitment of the EU to the principles of the European Convention and other international obligations that affect the freedom of the individual.

INDEX

TERMINOLOGY, 1, 100, 102–103
TIME LIMITS,
  annulment actions, 57
TORTIOUS LIABILITY OF
    COMMUNITY, 59–60
TRADEMARKS, 68, 76–77
TRAINING, 89
TRANS-EUROPEAN NETWORKS, 4
TRANSPORT POLICY, 4
TREATIES,
  See also Treaty of Amsterdam;
      Treaty on European Union;
      Treaty of Nice
  direct effect, 31–32
  EC Treaty, 20
  Merger Treaty, 1, 20
  preliminary references, 39
  sex discrimination, 95–98
  sources of community law, 19–20
  supremacy of Community law, 2
  Treaty of Rome, 20
TREATY OF AMSTERDAM, 19
  amendment of TEU, 1
  co-decision procedure, 4
  co-operation procedure, 4
  Commission, 10
  decision-making, 4
  European Parliament, 3
  reforms, 18
  Treaty on European Union (TEU),
      101–105
TREATY ON EUROPEAN UNION
    (TEU), 19, 20, 100–105
  acquis communautaire, 101–102
  amendment, 1
  assent procedure, 4
  border controls, 105
  citizenship, 103–104
  co-decision procedure, 4
  Commission, 101
  common commercial policy, 105
  common foreign and security
      policy, 104, 105
  Council of Ministers, 101
  crime, 105
  enlargement of the Union, 101
  entry into force, 1, 100
  European Council, 19
  European Parliament, 3, 101, 104
  fundamental rights, 103
  institutional changes, 101
  international crime, 105

TREATY ON EUROPEAN UNION
    (TEU)—*cont.*
  justice and home affairs, 105
  national identities, 103
  national parliaments, 103
  numbering, 100
  Ombudsman, 104
  ratification, 100
  Schengen Convention, 105
  sex discrimination, 99
  subsidiarity, 102, 103
  terminology, 1, 100, 102–103
  three pillars, 104–105
  Treaty of Amsterdam, 101–105
  Treaty of Rome, 102–103
TREATY OF NICE, 19, 105–107
  amendment of TEU, 1
  approval, 105
  closer co-operation, 107
  co-decision procedure, 4, 106
  Commission, 106–107
  Council of Ministers, 106
  Court of First Instance, 15, 107
  enlargement of the Union, 106
  European Court of Justice, 107
  European Parliament, 3, 106
  ratification, 106
  reforms, 18
TREATY OF ROME, 20
  Treaty on European Union (TEU),
      102–103
TRIBUNALS,
  preliminary references, 40–41
"TRUE EUROPEANS", 18

VALIDITY ACTIONS, 40, 47
VERTICAL DIRECT EFFECT, 32–33,
    34–36
VETOES,
  Council of Ministers, 8
VISAS, 80
VOCATIONAL COURSES,
  free movement of workers, 79
VOCATIONAL TRAINING, 89
VON COLSON PRINCIPLE, 36
VOTING,
  Council of Ministers, 7
  European Council, 4

WELFARE SCHEMES, 97, 98
WORKERS. *See* FREE MOVEMENT
    OF WORKERS

Notes

Notes